The Poetry of

GABRIEL CELAYA

THE POETRY
OF
GABRIEL CELAYA

Translated by Betty Jean Craige

LEWISBURG
BUCKNELL UNIVERSITY PRESS
LONDON AND TORONTO: ASSOCIATED UNIVERSITY PRESSES

Associated University Presses
440 Forsgate Drive
Cranbury, NJ 08512

Associated University Presses
25 Sicilian Avenue
London WC1A 2QH, England

Associated University Presses
2133 Royal Windsor Drive
Unit 1
Mississauga, Ontario
Canada L5J 1K5

Library of Congress Cataloging in Publication Data

Celaya, Gabriel, 1911–
 . The poetry of Gabriel Celaya.

  English and Spanish.
  Includes index.
  1. Spanish poetry—20th century—Translations into
English. 2. English poetry—Translations from Spanish.
I. Craige, Betty Jean. II. Title.
PQ6623.U34A23 1984   861'.64   83-45367
ISBN 0-8387-5062-1

Printed in the United States of America

To Coates (Dick) Johnson

Contents

Contents

Acknowledgments

I would like to thank Begoña Bilbao Canup for her time and effort in checking my versions of Celaya's poems for their "accuracy," and I would like to thank Gabriel Celaya for his cooperation and enthusiasm for the project.

Introduction

Fi-4

Man has not died.
Only an image.
That of human man
who thought himself someone.
Since that image has gone
I can sing in peace:
Calmly I shall speak
the words of Sir No One,
without crying for
him who exists not.
I can thus
combine my words
in an inexpressive mode,
a systematic, neutral mode.
I can always, as they say,
be correct once more,
and if necessary in the end
write a sonnet.
But . . .

Gabriel Celaya, author of *Chamber Lyric (Lírica de cámara)*, which contains "Fi-4" and other "posthumanist" poems, is a Basque poet from San Sebastián, Spain, whose recent poetry articulates the implications for mankind of the end of the dualist paradigm. In this book, which takes its title from the Wilson cloud chamber (developed by the Nobel laureate physicist C. T. Wilson for the study of ionized particles), Celaya presents, enthusiastically, the universe of colliding subatomic particles in which man is nothing special, since he is not intrinsically distinct from other systems of atoms. When we recognize such a universe where there is no spiritual realm, no God, to give man a soul—to make man special—then we must accept the here and now as all we have and in calmness speak "the words of Sir No One," without crying in anguish for what does not exist. But, says Celaya in the preface to "Fi-4," "it is so difficult to extricate oneself from humanist madness!"

Celaya, born in 1911 in the province of Guipúzcoa as Rafael Gabriel Múgica Celaya, published his first book *Tide of Silence* (*Marea del silencio*, 1935) under the name of Rafael Múgica. It was a volume of surrealist poetry which did not please his family. Because his literary endeavors separated him from those who expected him to work for the family company in San Sebastián, the poet decided to change his name, choosing for a brief time to use "Juan de Leceta" and then for the rest of his life "Gabriel Celaya." In the course of his career he moved from surrealism through existentialism to posthumanism, finally writing poems about language as the source of the thoughts we once believed to be our own.

Celaya has spent most of his life either in San Sebastián, in the north of Spain, or in Madrid, where he lived for eight years at the Residencia de Estudiantes while attending the University and where he lives now with his companion of almost forty years, Amparo Gastón. In 1947, while still residing in San Sebastián, he worked with her to establish a publishing house called Colección de Poesía "Norte," through which he published not only several books of his own poetry but also translations of William Blake's *The Book of Urizen* and Rimbaud's *Une Saison en enfer*, and through which he published the "social" poetry of many young writers, some of them in exile, who did not support the Franco regime. Throughout the years Celaya has been politically active, by writing and by offering himself as a candidate of the Basque Communist Party for a seat in Las Cortes (which he did not win). He has published over fifty books of poetry, as well as several novels, translations, and long critical essays.[1]

Celaya's work should be of interest to readers of late-twentieth-century poetry as well as to scholars of contemporary thought, because in its various stages it marks the shift from the humanist model of reality (Cartesian dualism), with its confidence in the possibility of objective representation of the world, to the relativist model, with its cultural self-consciousness. Our century undergoes this philosophical shift as we come to recognize that the order we once believed to inhere in an objectively definable external reality is to some extent man-made and culturally specific: the values we once thought intrinsic to phenomena now disclose themselves to

1. See Sharon Keefe Ugalde, *Gabriel Celaya* (Boston: Twayne, 1978), pp. 11–28.

16

be man-given rather than God-given. The philosophical revolution accompanies both the scientific revolution of relativity and the aesthetic revolution of cubism and surrealism, all of which call attention to *point of view* in their fundamental assumption that our point of view governs our knowledge of reality at any given time.

Celaya's early poetry of *Marea del silencio* is apparently subjectivist in nature, as is all surrealist poetry and painting, for surrealism explores the psyche—through dreams, through the imagination—in search of a super reality beyond that reality ordinarily perceptible through our five senses. We can see in such poems as "The Moon" both the irrational association of images that belongs to the surrealist rebellion against discursive language and thought and the belief that what we see reflects what is in our minds. It concludes:

> This is enough: to know
> that if I see fish
> pass through the transparent moon,
> they reflect only
> the ones passing slowly
> through my icy gold eyes.

The moon, forever beyond reach, serves the poet as a mirror, causing him to watch himself, as he says in the second stanza, "in the still waters of [his] thought." But that personal self-reflection does not diminish a longing for a beyond, for a supernatural reality which the surrealists tried to reveal through automatic writing or the coupling of unusual images.

In presenting a possible escape from the dualist isolation of the rational self by (theoretically) suppressing the functioning of the conscious ego, surrealism contributed to the decline of humanism. Humanism exalted the individual and the individual's capacity for accurate observation of the natural world, and it thus postulated an isolable self somehow independent of the physical phenomena, including the body, that the self observed rationally. It generated the aesthetic of representation, or realism. Surrealism abandoned that dichotomy of self and world by questioning the boundaries of the self or ego and by reaching into the unconscious for images that issued out of the collective mind of mankind. And it abandoned the realist aesthetic. If surrealism's emphasis on the unconscious processes of the mind allows us to locate the movement at the close of humanism's domination of Western thought, however, its attention to language allows us to link it with the beginnings of posthumanism. Surrealism's employment of nondiscursive syntax and illogical image patterns worked to bring to the twentieth century an awareness of the role language plays in shaping our perception, an awareness that leads ultimately to the nonsubjectivist, poststructuralist assumption that the language we inherit and use gives us both the limitations and the possibilities of our thought.

Dualism plays itself out in our culture when man recognizes that his separation of spirit from matter, or self from world, leads to the perception of nothingness within the self and meaninglessness without. The belief in an isolable self implies a belief in a transcendent spiritual reality, and man's demand for that spiritual reality makes him forever unfulfilled, forever dissatisfied with the material world at hand, forever suffering romantic longing. According to posthumanist thinking, the desire for something beyond created God in the first place, and when man lost belief in God, that desire created man's feeling of isolation and abandonment in the now empty universe. The same desire directed inward produced man's feeling of emptiness within.

By comparing two of Celaya's more recent poems, we can see the poet's shift from a desire for a transcendent reality to the knowledge that Western man has created that desire by his particular metaphysical model of reality. By 1960 Celaya had left surrealism far behind, and he used a more discursive language in his poem "The Old Man and the Sea," which he called a "gloss on Hemingway." In the poem the old fisherman went out to sea and suddenly faced "the unnamable, the light with intangible tail," which represented for him "a possible glory;" when he lost the fish to savage birds, he knew he had lost something special that the sea had given him to glimpse—for a few moments only. And after his triumph the old man was sad. Celaya's fisherman was sad because he believed in a mysterious realm beyond the natural world, a spiritual reality unavailable, except perhaps in rare mystical moments, to man locked within a material world.

In 1976 Celaya published a poem whose Spanish title is "La Lata (de vivir)," an inadequate translation of which is "The Can (of Living)." The poem plays on the word *lata*, which means both tin can, of the sort we use for preserving food, and annoyance or frustration. The poem begins:

> He opens and empties a can.
> He puts the can opener inside.
> Then he closes the can, soldering it well,
> and hides it where it cannot be found.
> Later he gets on a boat
> and leaves.
> He will search for the can opener he's hidden in the can,
> in the can he's hidden by tossing it in the sea,

thinking, transcendentally,
"What good is a can opener
that is not hard to find?"

Celaya's poem is really about the dualist definition of man, and it offers a way out of the despair of the fisherman: it shows as man-made the "mystery" which is the object of man's longing. In the second half of the poem, the poet says that this action of locking the can opener within the can and losing the can within the sea is the "lata" of existence, the problem that human beings cannot avoid, "because it's hard to believe that the here and now is more than the beyond." Now that man cannot open the can, which he cannot even find, he must open it, for it contains its secret, which man thinks he must have. And because man cannot obtain that can opener, he feels incomplete.

When man becomes aware that he makes his own tragic sensibility, within his culture, then he can laugh at the order of things that is man-made. For when man ceases to postulate a beyond that would give transcendent meaning to the here and now, he has to acknowledge that all the values he once thought inherent in phenomena, in an "external reality," are given by culture.

Now that we can watch ourselves make order we can watch our culture make us. We lose the humanist belief in an autonomous self when we see that our consciousness is constructed by the network of social, psychological, ideological, and linguistic systems in which we participate within our particular culture. So we lose our belief in free will, the free will which, as Sartre said, made us responsible for "ourselves and therefore for all men," the free will which made us responsible for all our choices; now we see that our thoughts and social practices are constrained, in a complex way, by language. So we lose our belief in originality.

Celaya says in the concluding lines of another recent poem:

We are the voice of no one.
We are never we but rather that other in us
possessed by the nothingness of the delirious no one.

Being the voice of no *one,* never our*selves* but rather the otherness in us ("lo otro en nos*otros*"), we relinquish our once passionate faith in our own individuality. We come to believe, as Roland Barthes argues in "The Death of the Author," that the author of a text is not an original thinker externalizing his thoughts through language but instead is a writer "born simultaneously with his text." The notion that our thoughts are those of the texts of our culture does not

19

disturb Celaya, for in his acceptance of a world without a transcendent beyond to endow us with isolable selves capable of original ideas he finds a pleasure, which is that of the poet's participation in the culture's consciousness. In "Poetry, Inc.," he says:

> Perfect future! There's no other permanence
> than that of an echo corrected by those
> who won't know my name or adventure—I hope.
> Neither do I know who speaks in my conscience.

Few Spaniards have been heard in the recent international discussion on what Derrida calls the "decentered universe," a discussion dominated in fact by the Frenchmen Barthes, Foucault, and Derrida himself. Celaya is an unusual Spanish poet, well-known in his country, who deserves attention outside Spain for producing a body of poetry expressive of man's new understanding of his place in the universe—that is, his new posthumanist understanding of nature in which man is not central, not special. His intellectual journey from humanism to posthumanism, which he made by way of learning of the Wilson chamber, is the journey that intellectuals in many other disciplines have taken in their efforts to explain human reality in a way consistent with the knowledge of nature we have gained through the physical sciences. As Celaya says in "Fi-4," he could still "write a sonnet. But . . ."

A Note on the Translation

A poem is a "little whore," according to Celaya, for each reader knows it and loves it in a different way. Because "every worthy poem is transformed on others' lips," Celaya acknowledges that a poem will be repeated, remembered, misremembered, and even misunderstood, when it leaves the poet to belong to everyone. So perhaps Celaya will understand the translator's role, which is to bring a poem that traveled widely in its own country into the translator's land, where it will look different, just as the world itself looks different in each language. The translator too is a lover of the poem; and even though he knows that his own language is never adequate to reproduce either the poetry or the shape the world takes in the poem, he wants to introduce it to his friends, to people who cannot know it in its own culture.

To translate a large number of poems by a single poet is to establish that poet's identity for readers who cannot know the poet's work directly. The translator's words carry a baggage of sense and association distinct from that of the poet's words; and the poet's words, laden with the allusions and echoes, sounds and syllables, rhymes and rhythms that delighted his readers, disappear. In fact, the whole corpus of the original poetry disappears, to be replaced in the translator's language by a selection of poems the translator makes according to his own and his culture's literary taste and ideology. So a new image of the poet is fashioned by the translator's choice and presentation.

In selecting these poems by Celaya to translate into English, I have become aware of how the interests of a translator govern the translation. I decided to do the project because I found in Celaya's recent work—that of *Lírica de cámara* and later—an articulation of the relativist paradigm that I also find (and like) in the writings of the poststructuralist philosophers. Because it is this posthumanist

21

poetry that I find most interesting—particularly in a Spanish (Basque) poet—I have translated more of it than of the earlier poetry. If this selection presents Celaya as a philosopher-poet of the relativist paradigm, rather than as a love poet (and Celaya certainly wrote many love poems), than I take responsibility for giving him that image in the English-speaking community; for I believe it is the philosopher-poet Celaya who will be most exciting to us.

Finally, I must state my philosophy of translation. As a translator, I have always endeavored to stay as close to the original as possible in selecting "equivalent" words, expressions, and tones for those of the Spanish poetry, in order to give the English-speaking reader some knowledge of the poet's way of putting reality together. If my goal had been different, I might have made flashier or more "beautiful" poems, but then they would have been more my own and even less Celaya's. Celaya uses an uncomplicated syntax and vocabulary, and so do I in my translation, exercising freedom in my reproduction of his poems only when I feel that the rhyme or rhythm of the Spanish demands translation as much as the words. Celaya's poetry has indeed stepped out on the street, as Celaya says of the poem in "The Poem Kisses Everyone," and I hope that the version I have provided here will make English-speaking readers stop to take a look at this Spanish representative of posthumanism.

The Poetry of
GABRIEL CELAYA

Las Poesías

The Poems

Pasarán gaviotas veloces, altas gaviotas

Pasarán gaviotas veloces, altas gaviotas,
sobre casas de cristal, terrazas de cristal,
donde muchachas blancas
tocan los pianos de cristal.

Pasará una brisa de algas y mar
por el pinar de cristal,
por las grandes avenidas,
por las calles,
por las plazas
de la ciudad de cristal.

Pasará una brisa leve
mientras las blancas muchachas
mueven sus brazos en alto y a compás.

Pasarán nubes lentas y blancas
por el cielo de cristal,
sobre mares de cristal,
cuando muchachas blancas entornando los ojos
hagan con su silencio la hora de cristal.

Por el aire transparente,
por mis ojos transparentes,
pasarán las lentas nubes del silencio,
las gaviotas del gozo,
la brisa,
lo eterno.

Y habrá blancas muchachas en el aire y en mis ojos,
y habrá un gozo sin sentido,

*From *Marea del silencio.*

Swift Gulls Will Pass, High Flying Gulls

Swift gulls will pass, high flying gulls,
over houses of glass, terraces of glass,
where white girls play
the pianos of glass.

A breeze of seaweed and ocean will pass
through the pine grove of glass,
through the great avenues,
through the streets,
through the plazas
of the city of glass.

A light breeze will pass
while the white girls in rhythm
move their arms up and down.

Slow white clouds will pass
through the sky of glass,
over oceans of glass,
when white girls half shutting their eyes
form with their silence the hour of glass.

Through the transparent air,
through my transparent eyes,
the slow clouds of silence will pass,
the gulls of delight,
the breeze,
the eternal.

And there will be white girls in the air and in my eyes,
and there will be senseless delight,

y un olor de inmensidad,
y frente al mar infinito
habrá terrazas, pinares,
una ciudad de cristal.

Sonámbulo

Como un buzo sumergido
en la profundidad submarina del misterio,
avanzaba el sonámbulo, lentísimo como el miedo,
por el fondo de su sueño.

Recorría calles de mármol,
inmensas plazas solitarias,
soportales y andenes
de las grandes ciudades deshabitadas.

Solo comprendía
los timbres que suenan precipitadamente,
las voces tartamudas y electrocutadas
de los teléfonos que comunican con la muerte.

Astronomía del sueño
eran sus movimientos.
La eternidad le envolvía:
¡música del silencio!

*From *Marea del silencio*.

Angeles verdes

Angeles verdes,
ángeles sabios,
paseaban serenos por los prados

*From *Marea del silencio*.

and immensity's scent,
and by the infinite sea
there will be terraces, pines,
a city of glass.

Sleepwalker

Like a diver submerged
in the sea bottom's mystery
the sleepwalker advanced, as slowly as fear,
through the depths of his dream.

He walked marble streets,
immense empty plazas,
platforms and porticos
of the great abandoned cities.

Alone he understood
the chimes sounding in haste,
the stuttering, electrocuted voices
of the phones communicating with death.

The steps he took
made dream's astronomy.
Eternity enveloped him:
Music of silence!

Green Angels

Green angels,
wise angels,
they would calmly cross the fields

con una flor de plata en la boca
y un compás en la mano.

Angeles del aire verde,
ángeles eléctricos,
ángeles de cristal y de acero,
ángeles.

Con sus dedos metálicos y delgados
entreabrían los párpados
de las estatuas
y les miraban absortos y en silencio
aquellos ojos ciegos,
inertes,
vueltos al blanco misterio de lo eterno.

Onda del silencio

Entre la vida y el sueño
sube y baja el silencio.

Sube con la tarde, pura
de penúltimas nostalgias amarillas;
baja con la noche, lenta
de alas y muertos de espuma.

Entre la vida y el sueño
sube y baja el silencio.

Sube con el dedo quieto
sobre sus labios morados;
baja lento a sus abismos
con los ojos entornados

Sube y anuncia:
¿qué anuncia?
Baja y me dice:
¿qué dice?

*From *Marea del silencio.*

30

All the Roses Incarnate with Desire Are Here!

All the roses incarnate with desire are here!
the moon is there, still,
white, sterile, watching,
a mirror turned into itself,
Narcissus' perfection:
solitude in white waters
of the quiet, cold white.

Hard or bloodless, calm,
it is watching itself,
while incarnate live roses,
of flesh and of love,
faint with pleasure
beneath a hot breeze.

With my eyes on the moon,
red roses under my feet,
quiet, I am waiting
for you, for myself
to come to you over your shoulder
with a white and green
kiss of silence;
for you, for myself to come to you
with a kiss
dead for its pure perfection.

The Moon

The moon.
What a mirror, blind,
turned forever to itself!
The moon, pure and round,
naked in the waters of silence!

Me quedo pálido y alto,
y mi música se mueve con la música del cielo.
Me quedo blanco, callado,
contemplándome en las aguas
quietas de mi pensamiento.

Esto me basta: saber
que si veo cruzar peces
por el fondo de la luna transparente,
serán tan solo el reflejo
de aquellos que pasan lentos
por el fondo de mis ojos de oro y hielo.

Es la hora de las raíces y los perros amarillos

Es la hora de las raíces y los perros amarillos.
El hombre se pone como una máscara su silencio;
se le llenan los ojos de yedra.

Es la hora de las raíces y los perros amarillos;
la hora en que blanquísimos caballos
pasan como escalofríos por el fondo de la niebla.

Oigo como una ausencia que el misterio está muy cerca;
oigo como una música
que la noche vuelve la cabeza.

Es la hora de las raíces y los perros amarillos;
en su sala de cristal,
la luna llora con la cabeza entre las manos.
El hombre se pone como una máscara su silencio;
sueña en el fondo del agua.

Es la hora del escalofrío en los cuerpos desnudos,
la hora en que se llora el misterio que viene y que no viene;
la luna es el dolor de esa ausencia
ante los crueles y apretados dientes blancos de los hombres.

Es la hora de las raíces y los perros amarillos,

*From *Marea del silencio*.

36

I stand pale and tall,
and my music moves with the sky's.
I stand white and still,
watching myself
in the still waters of my thought.

This is enough: to know
that if I see fish
pass through the transparent moon,
they reflect only
the ones passing slowly
through my icy gold eyes.

It's the Hour of Roots and Yellow Dogs

It's the hour of roots and yellow dogs.
Man dons his silence like a mask;
his eyes fill with ivy.

It's the hour of roots and yellow dogs;
the hour when whitest horses
like shivers pass through the depths of the mist.

I hear like an absence that the mystery is close;
I hear like a melody
that night turns its head.

It's the hour of roots and yellow dogs;
in their crystal hall
the moon cries head in hand.
Man dons his silence like a mask;
he dreams in the depths of the water.

It's the hour of the shiver on naked bodies,
the hour of crying for the mystery that does and does not come;
the moon is the pain of that absence
before the cruel, clenched white teeth of men.

It's the hour of roots and yellow dogs,

de las raíces transparentes en el fondo de las aguas,
de los perros locos huyendo
por salas grandes y blancas.

Es la hora del misterio que viene y que no viene,
la hora en que la noche huye del mar desnuda,

la hora en que de cada estatua se escapan todos los pájaros,
la hora de los párpados de plata,
la hora en que la luna murmura como un silencio:
nada.

En el fondo de la noche

En el fondo de la noche tiemblan las aguas de plata.
La luna es un grito muerto en los ojos delirantes.
Con su nimbo de silencio
pasan los sonámbulos de cabeza de cristal,
pasan como quien suspira,
pasan entre los hielos transparentes y verdes.

Es el momento de las rosas encarnadas y los puñales de acero
sobre los cuerpos blanquísimos del frío.

En el fondo de la noche tiembla el árbol del silencio;
los hombres gritan tan alto que sólo se oye a la luna.

Es el momento en que los niños se desmayan sobre los pianos,
el momento de las estatuas en el fondo transparente de las aguas,
el momento en que por fin todo parece posible.
En el fondo de la noche tiembla el árbol del silencio.

Decidme lo que habéis visto los que estabais con la cabeza vuelta.
La quietud de esta hora es un silencio que escucha,
el silencio es el sigilo de la muerte que se acerca.

Decidme lo que habéis visto.
En el fondo de la noche
hay un escalofrío de cuerpos ateridos.

*From *Marea del silencio*.

of transparent roots in the depths of the waters,
of mad dogs fleeing
through great white halls.

It's the hour of the mystery that does and does not come,
the hour when night flees the sea naked,

the hour when the birds fly away from every statue,
the hour of the eyelids of silver,
the hour when the moon murmurs like a silence:
nothing.

In the Depth of Night

In the depth of night ripple the silver waters.
The moon is a dead cry in delirious eyes.
Sleepwalkers with heads of glass
pass with their halos of silence,
pass like the taking of a breath,
pass through green, transparent frosts.

It is the moment of incarnate roses and daggers of steel
on bodies white with cold.

In the depth of night quivers the tree of silence;
men cry out so loudly only the moon is heard.

It is the moment when children faint on pianos,
the moment of statues in the water's transparent depths,
the moment at last when all looks possible.
In the depth of night quivers the tree of silence.

Tell me what you've seen, you who turned your heads.
The calm of the hour is a silence that hears,
the silence is the seal of the death that nears.

Tell me what you've seen.
In the depth of night
there's a chill of bodies stiff from cold.

La Brisa pasa como una música

La brisa pasa como una música por el fondo de la tarde.
Yo soy un árbol de cristal bajo las aguas transparentes,
la mano del misterio que se mueve en el silencio.

Yo soy lo que se ignora:
el estremecimiento de luz que precede a la aparición de las
    espadas;
yo soy eso, solo eso;
yo espero lo que esperan
esos cinco hombres mudos, tristes, sentados en un salón de
    terciopelo morado.

Al atardecer suenan clarines de oro.
Un león de llamas huye por el fondo del bosque;
la virgen de ojos verdes se cubre el rostro con las manos.

Es mi momento, el último momento:
cuando la luz rompe los cristales nada más tocarlos con la yema de
    los dedos;
cuando huye el pájaro vivo encerrado en las blancas clausuras de
    lo abstracto;
cuando uno de los hombres del salón morado dice a los otros:
"Ya no puede tardar."

Es el último momento.
Me deslizo al filo de un silencio que casi es la muerte.
La virgen de ojos verdes me muestra la más peligrosa de sus
    sonrisas.

Es el último momento.
Estalla el oro morado del crepúsculo;
las raíces de la carne me duelen;
siento como un temblor que me hago transparente.

Es el último momento:
la muerte pasa muy cerca murmurando sus secretos;
es entonces
cuando las estatuas son el sueño del silencio

*From *Marea del silencio*.

The Breeze Passes like a Melody

The breeze passes like a melody through the deep afternoon.
I am a glass tree beneath transparent waters,
the hand of the mystery that moves in the silence.

I am the unknown:
the quiver of light before the appearance of swords;
I am that, that alone;
I await what those five men await,
sitting in a purple velvet parlor, sad and mute.

At dusk the gold bugles sound.
A flaming lion flees through deep woods;
the green-eyed virgin hides her face in her hands.

It is my moment, the final moment:
when light shatters glass at the fingertip's touch;
when the caged bird flees the white cloisters of the abstract;
when one of the purple parlor's men says to the others:
"It won't be long now."

It is the final moment:
I slip on the edge of a silence almost death.
The green-eyed virgin shows me her most dangerous smile.

It is the final moment.
The purple gold of the twilight bursts;
the roots of my flesh begin to hurt;
I feel a shudder that turns me transparent.

It is the final moment:
murmuring her secrets, death passes near;
it is then
when the statues are silence's dream

y los pianos
huelen como un niño muerto entre los lirios.

Es el último momento,
cuando da miedo volver la cabeza,
cuando parece que lo comprendemos todo y, sin embargo, no
     sabemos nada;
cuando uno de los hombres del salón morado, quieto ante el
     balcón,
mira hacia el espejo con los ojos en blanco.

La Luna pasa como un escalofrío

La luna pasa como un escalofrío entre las estatuas de mármol,
les habla al oído de la muerte,
las acaricia con sus manos de goma perfumada de éter,
mientras la noche se derrumba por dentro de sí misma.

Dos estatuas que se miran frente a frente tensan el silencio,
tienden los hilos invisibles de la trampa;
si un hombre se para entre ellas está perdido:
entra en un silencio del que ya no se sale,
un silencio dulcísimo, la muerte;
eso tensan dos estatuas que se miran frente a frente.

Narciso ha avanzado demasiado por dentro de sí mismo.
¿Qué ha visto en lo más hondo de su propio vacío?
Su amor es la voluptuosa languidez de la nada;
su amor es eso, la muerte,
lo que cantan tristemente las estatuas en la noche desmayada.

*From *Marea del silencio*.

and the pianos
smell like a child dead in the lilies.

It is the final moment:
when one is afraid to turn one's head,
when we seem to understand and yet know nothing;
when one of the purple parlor's men, quiet in front of the
    balcony,
looks toward the mirror with the whites of his eyes.

The Moon Passes like a Chill

The moon passes like a chill through the marble statues;
she speaks in their ears of death,
caresses them with hands scented with ether,
while the night collapses on itself.

Two facing statues tighten the silence,
stretch out the invisible threads of the trap;
if a man stops between them he is lost forever:
he enters a silence with no escape,
a sweet silence, death,
which the facing statues hold tight.

Narcissus has gone too far into himself.
In the depths of his emptiness what has he seen?
His love is the voluptuous languor of the void;
his love is death,
of which the statues sing sadly in the swooning night.

La Luna es una loca que pasea

La luna es una loca que pasea
por las largas galerías de cristal de su palacio;
lleva en una mano una espada de plata
y apretado entre los dientes un limón ácido y frío.

La luna decapita cisnes blandos y niños.
¿No oís en la noche su blanquísima espada
segar rápida y suave los quietos silencios?

La luna es una loca
que, sentada ante el mar, canta
mientras peina su larga cabellera
de luz fría y delgada.

La luna es . . .
—¡silencio!, ¡silencio!—
la luna y una espada.

*From *Marea del silencio*.

La Luna piensa la ausencia

La luna piensa la ausencia
de lo que yo estoy buscando.
Las aguas claras, absortas,
sueñan el cuerpo de una virgen desnuda
tranquilamente dormida en el fondo transparente;
la luna piensa un silencio
mientras los hombres la miran con ojos de pez muerto,
mientras mi pensamiento sueña la eternidad del ser.

Camino así perdido por una gran nada blanca.
Mis gritos en la nieve se hacen árboles de cristal,
mientras la muerte canta dulcemente, muy lejos, en lo hondo,

*From *Marea del silencio*.

The Moon Is a Mad Woman Who Promenades

The moon is a mad woman who promenades
along her palace's glass corridors;
in her teeth she holds a cold, tart lemon,
in her hand a silver sword.

The moon beheads soft swans and children.
Don't you hear her swift white sword in the night
smooth as it reaps the silent calm?

The moon is a mad woman
who sings at the seaside
and combs her flowing hair
of cold and delicate light.

The moon is . . .
—silence! silence!—
the moon and a sword.

The Moon Thinks the Absence

The moon thinks the absence
of what I am seeking.
The clear waters dream
the body of a naked virgin
calmly asleep in the transparent depths;
the moon thinks a silence
while men gaze at her with dead fish eyes,
while my thought dreams the eternity of being.

Thus I walk lost in a great white void.
My cries in the snow become glass trees,
while death sings sweetly, far away, deep,

o mueve ante los ojos dilatados del espanto
sus siete espadas trémulas de luces.

La muerte es una virgen desnuda
bañándose en los verdes estanques de la luna;
la muerte es el vacío que me envuelve
cuando recorro un paisaje de nieve;
la muerte es el silencio.
¿No lo veis a esa hora en que el mar es un toro dormido en la
        última playa?

El Espejo me refleja

El espejo me refleja, me vuelve hacia mí mismo.
Lentamente me hundo en mis pálidos abismos.
Me veo reflejado, ya, desde muy lejos,
perdido en esa blanca catedral del silencio
donde la luna es la virgen desnuda y muerta que yo adoro.

La noche tiende sus trampas invisibles:
el que se asoma a un espejo está cogido,
le sorprenden los misterios imprevistos,
se pierde en un laberinto de cristales y espejos giratorios.

En el fondo del silencio la muerte es un río lento;
yo lo miro pasar de la luna al azogue;
mientras alguien apoya sus dedos helados sobre las yemas de mis
        dedos,
no sé qué me mueve a sonreír tristemente.

Alguien me lleva de la mano por el borde de los precipicios;
un amor, un delirio, el vértigo me llama;
el espanto es el más dulce de los escalofríos
cuando crece súbitamente como un árbol en el fondo de la carne.

Me miro fijamente en el espejo:
la noche me ha cogido en sus trampas sutiles.
Me siento cada vez más hondo:
la muerte se inclina sobre mí para besarme.

From La Soledad cerrada.

46

or moves her seven swords aquiver with light
in front of eyes grown wide with fright.

Death is a naked virgin
bathing in the moon's green pools;
death is the emptiness around me
when I travel a landscape of snow;
death is silence.
Don't you see it when the sea is a bull asleep on the last shore?

The Mirror Reflects Me

The mirror reflects me, turns me into myself.
Slowly I sink into the dim cavern within.
I see my reflection, already from afar,
lost in the white cathedral of silence,
where the moon is the naked, dead virgin I adore.

Night lays out its invisible traps:
whoever appears in the mirror is caught,
surprised by mysteries he wouldn't foresee,
lost in a labyrinth of revolving mirrors and glass.

Death's a slow river in silence's depths;
I watch it run by from the moon to the pool;
while someone rests frozen fingers in mine,
I know not what moves me sadly to smile.

Someone takes me by the hand to the cliff's edge;
a love, a delirium, a vertigo calls;
of all the chills the sweetest is fear
when it springs up like a tree in the depths of the flesh.

I stare into the mirror at myself:
night has caught me in its subtle traps.
Deeper and deeper I feel myself sink:
death leans over for a kiss.

Me dan miedo esos ojos, mis dos ojos sin nubes
que desde el espejo me miran implacables
mientras baten espadas de luz
en sus aguas heladas y azules.

Amor

Vivir es fácil y, a veces, casi alegre.

Esta tarde—mar, pinares, azul—,
suspendido entre los brazos ligerísimos del aire
y entre los tuyos, dulce, dulce mía,
un ritmo palpitante me cantaba:
vivir es fácil y, a veces, casi alegre.

La brisa unía en un mismo latido
nuestros cuerpos, los árboles, las olas,
y nosotros no éramos distintos
de las nubes, los pájaros, los pinos,
de las plantas azules de agua y aire,
plantas, al fin, nosotros, de callada y dulce carne.

La tierra se extasiaba; ya casi era divina
en las nubes redondas, en la espuma,
en este blanco amor que, radiante, se eleva
al suave empuje de dos cuerpos que se unen en la hierba.

¿Recuerdas, dulce mía, cuando el aire
se llenaba de palomas invisibles,
de una música o brisa que tu aliento
repetía apresurado de secretos?

Vivir es fácil y, a veces, casi alegre.
Contigo entre los brazos estoy viendo
caballos que me escapan por un aire lejano,
y estoy, y estamos, tocando con los labios
esas flores azules que nacen de la nada.

Vivir es fácil y, a veces, casi alegre.

From La Música y la sangre.

Those eyes frighten me, those cloudless eyes
that from the mirror stare without rest,
while in their icy blue water
clash swords of light.

Love

Living is easy and, at times, almost a joy.

This evening—sea, pine groves, blue—,
a rhythm carried in the arms of the wind
and in yours, my love,
was making its song felt in me:
living is easy and, at times, almost a joy.

The breeze united in a single beat
our bodies, the waves, and the trees,
and we were indistinguishable from
the clouds, the birds, and the pines,
the blue plants of water and air;
we had become plants ourselves, of sweet silent flesh.

The enraptured earth was almost divine
in the round clouds and the sea's foam,
in this radiant white love emerging with the thrust
of bodies made one in the grass.

Do you remember when the air was filled,
my love, with doves we couldn't see,
with a music, a breeze that your soft breath
when pressed by secrets would bring again?

Living is easy and, at times, almost a joy.
When I am in your arms I see
horses fleeing on a distant wind,
and I, we, touch with our lips
those blue blossoms born of the void.

Living is easy and, at times, almost a joy.

Al hablar, confundimos; al andar, tropezamos;
al besarnos no existe un solo error posible:
resucitan los cuerpos cantando, y parece
que vamos a cubrirnos de flores diminutas,
de flores blancas, lo mismo que un manzano.

Dulce, dulce mía, ciérrame los ojos,
deja que este aire inunde nuestros cuerpos;
seamos solamente dos árboles temblando
con lo mismo que en ellos ha temblado esta tarde.

Vivir es más que fácil; es alegre.
Por caminos difíciles hoy llego
a la simple verdad de que tú vives.

Sólo quiero el amor, el árbol verde
que se mueve en el aire levemente
mientras nubes blanquísimas escapan
por un cielo que es rosa, que es azul, que es gris y malva,
que es siempre lo infinito y no comprendo,
ni quiero comprender, porque esto basta:
¡amor, amor!, tus brazos y mis brazos,
y los brazos ligerísimos del aire que nos lleva,
y una música que flota por encima,
que oímos y no oímos,
que consuela y exalta:
¡amor también volando a lo divino!

Primera inocencia

Era en el tiempo de la inocencia,
cuando las muchachas
apenas distinguían el amor de la brisa,
cuando los hombres lloraban de verdad
porque ni el piano ni ningún otro instrumento nocturno se habían
    inventado,
ni a nadie se le había ocurrido todavía la música
o que el dolor pudiera ser caricia.

*From *Movimientos elementales.*

Speaking we misunderstand; walking we stumble;
but kissing we do not go wrong:
our bodies revive in song,
and we cover ourselves in blossoms, it seems,
in the white blossoms of the apple tree.

My love, my love, shut my eyes for me,
through our bodies let the breeze flow;
let's be those two trees that are quivering
with what made them quiver this evening.

Living is more than easy; it's a joy.
By difficult paths I have come today
to the simple truth by which you live.

I want only love, the tree that is green
and moving slightly in the wind,
while white clouds escape in flight
across a sky flowered blue and gray and pink,
forever the infinite, and I don't understand,
nor do I care, for this is enough:
love! your arms and mine,
and the light arms of the wind,
and a music floating above
that occasionally we hear,
that consoles and exalts:
love flying divine!

First Innocence

It was the time of innocence
when girls
could hardly know love from the breeze,
when men really wept,
as the piano and the other instruments of night,
and music,
and the awareness that pain could caress
had yet to be born.

Era en el tiempo de la inocencia.
Las horas no pasaban cogidas de la mano
en cadenas de cifras monótonas y neutras;
flotaban desmayadas, por lo diáfano sueltas,
y apenas si los días contenían tristeza,
y el tiempo era una forma
a la que nadie había puesto nombre todavía.

La luz al retirarse cerraba el ojo humano.
Nadie había explorado hacia dentro la noche.
Al hablar de Dios se le confundía con el mar
y en la atmósfera clara volaban
los gritos que, después, hemos llamado pensamientos
y las nubes
a las que no se acertaba a poner nombre preciso.

La aritmética era una planta blanca creciendo
en los ojos de un hombre enamorado del aire;
la música era un árbol mirándose en un río;
y los barcos
solamente existían en los cuentos.

El amor levantaba bandadas de palomas
que huían de lo oscuro o las ansias latentes,
y los hombres se hablaban dulcemente al oído
de una extraña presencia que llamaron silencio.

Dios sobre todo fue una obsesión terrible;
costó mucha inocencia perdida descubrirlo.
Al principio se hablaba solamente de un pájaro
y de un temblor que a veces se sentía en los labios.

Tiempos de agitación. Ya los poetas
gritaban en las plazas locamente
verdades y mentiras que también eran verdades.

La primera inocencia había muerto.
Los hombres se contaban con espanto su sueño.
Y alguien dijo entonces
que Dios ero lo uno, y la nada, y lo eterno.

It was the time of innocence,
The hours passed not hand-in-hand
in chains of monotonous, neutral numbers:
they floated unconscious, diaphanous, loose,
and the days could hardly hold sorrow,
and time was a form
no one had named.

The light as it faded shut mankind's eye.
No one had explored the inside of night.
When speaking of God they confused Him with the sea,
and in the clear air flew the cries
that later we have come to call thoughts
and the clouds
we had not yet named.

Arithmetic was a white plant growing
in the eyes of a man in love with the air;
music was a tree watching itself in a stream;
and boats
existed only in tales.

Love raised flocks of doves
that fled from the dark or from hidden desires,
and men spoke sweetly into each other's ears
of a strange presence they called silence.

God above all was a terrible obsession;
discovering Him cost their innocence.
At first they spoke only of a bird
and of a trembling they sometimes felt on their lips.

Tumultuous times. By now
the poets were shouting truths and truthful lies
madly in the city squares.

The first innocence had died.
Men spoke of their dream with fear.
And then someone said
that God was the whole, the nothingness, the eternal.

Ninfa

Se detiene en el borde del abismo y escucha,
viniendo desde el fondo, rampante, dulce, densa,
una serpiente alada, una música vaga.

Escapa por la suave pereza de su carne
que en el fondo era fango,
era ya tibia, y lenta, y latente, y sin forma;
era como el dios de gran barba dormido
junto al río en la siesta,
junto a ella en la noche·
carnal y sofocada de junio con olores.

Y escucha temblorosa,
apaga una tras otra penúltimas preguntas,
y duerme, se hunde, duerme
en brazos de un gran dios de pelo duro y rojo,
divino Pan: un dios
hecho bestia que huele.

*From *Movimientos elementales*.

La Fábula del río

La fábula del río (aquel anciano
de largas barbas verdes, húmedas y antiguas),
la fábula del aire luminoso
(espanto que encabrita los caballos),
la fábula primera en las orillas
de cierta desnudez que el agua siempre anuncia,
escuchaba yo, niño de arcilla roja y tierna.

Escuchaba. La escucho.
Me invades, ¿oh gran voz de una informe presencia!;
te siento por mis labios, levantándome, vaga;
te llamo río o veo

*From *Movimientos elementales*.

Nymph

She pauses at the edge of the abyss and listens,
raging, sweet, thick, emerging from the deep,
a winged serpent, a vague melody.

She escapes through the soft sloth of the flesh,
that deep within was mud;
it was formless, latent, warm, slow,
like the great bearded god
asleep beside the river in the afternoon,
beside her in the carnal night of June,
overwhelming in its fragrance.

And she listens, trembling,
silencing one question after another,
and then sleeps, sinking into the arms
of a great god with stiff red hair,
divine Pan: a god
made stinking beast.

The Legend of the River

The legend of the river (that old man
whose ancient wet beard is green and long),
the legend of bright hair
(the horror that makes horses rear),
the primal legend on the river's banks
of a nakedness the water always tells—
I heard it as a child of tender red clay.

I heard it. I hear it now.
You invade me, great voice of a presence everywhere!
I feel you on my lips, raising me up, vague;
I call you river, or I see

maravillosos mundos que sólo son palabras
mientras la calma augusta desciende con la siesta,
y hay juncos, y pereza, blando barro caliente.

¡Mitologías posibles! Infancia mía indemne,
antigua como el mundo y hoy, de pronto, presente!

Desde lo informe

Un dulce llanto espeso,
una delicia informe,
materia que me envuelve y sofoca en magnolias,
suave silencio oscuro,
aliento largo y blando.

Las caricias se espesan
(me derramo por ellas),
y voy por el jardín secreto, murmurando,
y, al tocarte, me asombro de que tengas un cuerpo,
y al alzar la cabeza,
las estrellas me asustan con su dura fijeza.

*From *Movimientos elementales*.

Posesión (1)

Si el sol sale, zumba, truena
como un dios antiguo de la luz poderosa,
hermoso, con sus barbas floridas y sus muslos
morenos, duros, recios,
también yo soy mujer,
también me abro en espasmo, pues eso es hacer versos:
llorar mientras resbalo por caricias y ríos
de sombra espesa y dulce.

*From *El Principio sin fin*.

fantastic worlds that are only words
while the magnificent calm descends with sleep,
and there are rushes, slowness, soft hot mud.

Possible myths! My childhood once protected,
ancient as the world and today, suddenly, here!

Out of the Formless

A sweet flood of tears,
a formless pleasure,
matter enfolding me, smothering me in magnolias,
a soft and dark silence,
a delicate, slow breathing.

The caresses increase
(I melt into them),
and I move through the secret garden, murmuring,
and when I touch you I am amazed you have a body,
and when I lift my head
I am frightened by the fixity of the stars.

Possession (1)

If the sun appears, it hums, and thunders
like an ancient god of powerful light,
beautiful, with flowered beard and dark thighs,
hard and strong;
I am woman too,
I too open in a spasm, for that is making poems,
crying as I slip on caresses and rivers
of thick, sweet shadow.

El Conocimiento

> Y conoció Adán a su mujer Eva.
> —*Genesis* 4

Porque el hombre es hombre busca,
combate seco, desgarra
una dulce materia femenina,
receptiva, sin forma, sin intención ni dueño.

Mas ellas son siempre suaves, siempre madres, y lloran
con su piedad difusa, su equívoca delicia,
su no pertenecerse totalmente a sí mismas.

Ellas esperan la gracia. Ellas perdonan, ofrecen
jardines y sonrisas—o la infancia: el descanso—,
ellas que flotan mecidas en un inefable encanto.

Mas nosotros, por hombres, cara a cara luchamos,
bien abiertos los ojos frente al vago infinito,
contra esas melodías que ablandan nuestros huesos.

Nosotros, bien definidos;
nosotros solos, macizos;
nosotros, en cuerpo entero consagrados a una empresa.

Que así, porque sí, nosotros,
contra equívocos, sonrisas, velos y vagos ensueños,
penetramos en su carne.
Las abrimos, las amamos para matar su secreto.

*From *El Principio sin fin*.

Final

La ironía nos desdobla.
El llanto puro nos funde

*From *Los Poemas de Juan de Leceta*.

58

Knowledge

And Adam knew his wife Eve.
—Genesis 4

Because man is man he seeks
and fights and tears
at the sweet receptive matter of woman,
that is without owner or purpose or form.

But women are always soft, maternal, and they cry
with their generous charity, their ambiguous delight,
their never belonging wholly to themselves.

They wait for grace. They forgive,
offer gardens and smiles—or rest for their infants—,
they float, rocked by an ineffable charm.

But we, because we're men, fight face to face,
our eyes wide open to the vague infinite,
against those melodies that soften our bones.

We men, well defined,
we men alone, solid;
we men, in our whole body devoted to one task.

So, because it's the way it is,
we men, against ambiguities, smiles, veils and vague dreams,
penetrate women's flesh.
we open them, we love them—to kill their secret.

The End

Irony splits us.
The pure sob fuses us

en la unidad sin conciencia,
en los días sin historia que aglomera el tiempo neutro.

Aquí acaban las palabras.
Queda solo este vagido,
queda esta mar, niño y viejo,
que se repite y chochea, ya aturdido, ya obstinado.

Y la aventura termina
en estas arenas lisas,
en este espacio que cruzan
largos vientos más que humanos, vastas ansias sin conciencia.

A Solas soy alguien

A solas soy alguien.
En la calle, nadie.

A solas medito,
siento que me crezco.
Le hablo a Dios. Responde
cóncavo el silencio.
Pero aguanta siempre,
firme frente al hueco,
este su seguro
servidor sin miedo.

A solas soy alguien,
valgo lo que valgo.
En la calle, nadie
vale lo que vale.

En la calle reinan
timbres, truenos, trenes
de anuncios y focos,
de absurdos peleles.
Pasan gabardinas,
pasan hombres "ene".

*From *Los Poemas de Juan de Leceta*.

in the oneness without consciousness,
in historyless days bound by neutral time.

Here words run out.
This wail alone remains,
this sea remains, child and old man,
repeating himself, doting, now stubborn, now dazed.

And the adventure ends
on this smooth sand,
in this space crossed
by winds more than human, vast longings without consciousness.

In Solitude I Am Someone

In solitude I am someone.
On the street, no one.

In solitude I muse.
I feel that I grow.
I speak to God.
The concave silence responds.
But his unfailing servant
endures ever firm
and ever without fear
in face of the void.

In solitude I am someone.
I am worth what I'm really worth.
On the street, no one
is worth what he's really worth.

On the street govern bells,
thunder, trains
of ads and headlights,
absurd mindless fools.
Gabardines go by,
and "n" number of men.

Todos son como uno,
pobres diablos: gente.

En la calle, nadie
vale lo que vale,
pero a solas, todos
resultamos alguien.

A solas existo,
a solas me siento,
a solas parezco
rico de secretos.
En la calle, todos
me hacen más pequeño
y al sumarme a ellos,
la suma da cero.

A solas soy alguien,
valgo lo que valgo.
En la calle, nadie
vale lo que vale.

A solas soy alguien,
entiendo a los otros.
Lo que existe fuera,
dentro de mí doblo.
En la calle, todos
nos sentimos solos,
nos sentimos nadie,
nos sentimos locos.

A solas soy alguien.
En la calle, nadie.

All are as one,
poor devils: people.

On the street, no one
is worth what he's really worth,
but in solitude everyone
becomes someone.

In solitude I exist,
in solitude I touch myself,
in solitude I seem
rich with secrets.
On the street, everyone
makes me smaller,
and when I add myself to them
the sum is zero.

In solitude I am someone,
I am worth what I'm really worth.
On the street, no one
is worth what he's really worth.

In solitude I am someone,
I understand others.
What exists outside myself
I double within.
On the street, everyone
feels all alone,
feels like no one,
feels almost insane.

In solitude I am someone.
On the street, no one.

Tranquilamente hablando

Puede reírse el mundo
con sus mandíbulas, con sus huesos,
su esqueleto batiente de rabia seca y dura,
con sarcasmo y aristas,
puede reírse, enorme, sin verme tan siquiera.
Porque estoy solo, y, solo,
yo lloro, no lo entiendo.

Pese al odio, al cansancio, las lágrimas, los dientes,
pese a las durezas de sangre congelada,
yo que pude seguirlo,
reírme como el mundo,
no lo entiendo—es sencillo—,
no entiendo su locura.

Si sube la marea,
si estoy en el balcón, y es de noche, y me crece
por dentro una ternura,
no lo entiendo, no entiendo
(debo ser algo tonto),
no entiendo esos ladridos y esa espuma del odio.

Serena noche, lenta
procesión de otros mundos,
vosotros que sabéis qué chiquito es mi pecho,
sabéis también que late,
que, triste, llama dentro
mi corazón sin nadie,
mi angustia sin destino,
mi sola soledad en medio de la risa.

*From *Los Poemas de Juan de Leceta.*

Speaking Calmly

The world may laugh
with its jaws, its bones,
its skeleton beating with dry, hard rage;
the enormous world, sarcastic and rough,
without even glimpsing me may laugh.
For I am alone, and lonely I cry—
I don't understand.

Despite the weariness and hate, the teeth and the tears,
despite the scabs of congealed blood,
I who once could go along with the world,
could laugh the way the world can laugh,
simply do not understand;
I don't understand its madness.

If the tide rises,
if I'm on my balcony, and it's night,
and a tenderness wells up within me,
I don't understand it, and I don't understand
(fool that I am)
the barking and the foaming of hate.

Peaceful night, slow
procession of other worlds,
you all who know how small is my chest,
know too how my heart beats,
calling sadly from within,
my heart alone,
my anguish without destiny,
my lonely solitude in the laughter.

Cuéntame cómo vives
(Cómo vas muriendo)

Cuéntame cómo vives;
dime sencillamente cómo pasan tus días,
tus lentísimos odios, tus pólvoras alegres
y las confusas olas que te llevan perdido
en la cambiante espuma de un blancor imprevisto.

Cuéntame cómo vives.
Ven a mí, cara a cara;
dime tus mentiras (las mías son peores),
tus resentimientos (yo también los padezco),
y ese estúpido orgullo (puedo comprenderte).

Cuéntame cómo mueres.
Nada tuyo es secreto:
la náusea del vacío (o el placer, es lo mismo);
la locura imprevista de algún instante vivo;
la esperanza que ahonda tercamente el vacío.

Cuéntame cómo mueres,
cómo renuncias—sabio—,
cómo—frívolo—brillas de puro fugitivo,
cómo acabas en nada
y me enseñas, es claro, a quedarme tranquilo.

*From *Se parece al amor.*

Ni más ni menos

Son tus pechos pequeños,
son tus ojos confusos,
lo que no tiene nombre
y no comprendo, adoro.

Son tus muslos largos

*From *Se parece al amor.*

Tell Me How You Live
(How You Die)

Tell me how you live;
tell me simply how you pass your days;
tell me of your slow hates, your moods of joy
and the bewildering waves where you're lost
in turbulent breakers you did not foresee.

Tell me how you live.
Come to me, face to face;
tell me your lies (mine are worse),
your resentments (that I suffer too),
and that stupid pride (I understand).

Tell me how you die.
Nothing of yours is secret:
the nausea of the void (or the pleasure, it's the same);
the unforeseen madness of some live moment;
the hope that stubbornly deepens the void.

Tell me how you die,
how—wisely—you become resigned,
how—frivolously—you briefly shine,
how in nothingness you end,
and you will teach me to be calm.

Neither More nor Less

Your eyes are puzzling,
your breasts are small,
what lacks a name
and I don't understand, I adore.

Your thighs are long

y es tu cabello corto;
lo que siempre me escapa
y no comprendo, adoro

Tu cintura, tu risa,
tus equívocos locos,
tu mirada que burla
y no comprendo, adoro.

¡Tú que estás tan cerca!
¡Tú que estás tan lejos!
Lo que beso, y no tengo,
y no comprendo, adoro.

En la otra orilla

Donde un agua quieta
espeja invirtiendo,
mas los lirios altos
apuntan lo bello,

donde eres tangible,
aunque no te entienda,
remoto, en la orilla
que abre a un mundo nuevo,

donde juveniles
y sin alma amamos,
donde la belleza,
ya no es ni consciente,

donde todo es visto,
mas nada está dicho,
yo, tranquilo, miro
el simple y extraño
ser que soy si amo.

*From *Se parece al amor.*

and your hair is short;
what escapes me always
and I don't understand, I adore.

Your laughter, your waist,
your crazy mistakes,
your mocking gaze—
and I don't understand, I adore

You who are so near!
You who are so far!
What I kiss and do not have
and I don't understand, I adore.

On the Other Shore

Where quiet waters
reflect the world inverted,
but the tall irises
point to the beautiful,

where I can touch you,
without understanding you,
remote on the shore
that opens to a new world,

where young and soulless
we love,
where beauty
is conscious no more,

where all is seen,
but nothing said,
in peace I gaze
at the simple and strange
being I am if I love.

En ti termino

Este objeto de amor no es objeto puro;
es un objeto bello, y creo que eso basta.
Bellos son sus brazos, sus hombros, sus senos;
bellos son sus ojos (¡y qué bien me mienten!).

Deseable, me engaña, o furtiva, resbala
suave, suavemente, con física dulzura,
o gravita hacia un centro más secreto que el alma;
o duele con un fuego más real que el cariño.

Si la beso, no hablo; si la toco, no creo;
y me quedo callado mirándola muy cerca,
o me duermo en sus brazos, o me muero en su espasmo,
y en aniquilarme hallo cierto descanso.

*From *Paz y concierto.*

Despedida

Quizá, cuando me muera,
dirán: "Era un poeta."
Y el mundo, siempre bello, brillará sin conciencia.

Quizá tú no recuerdes
quién fui, mas en ti suenen
los anónimos versos que un día puse en ciernes.

Quizá no quede nada
de mí, ni una palabra,
ni una de estas, parabras que hoy sueño en el mañana.

Pero visto o no visto,
pero dicho o no dicho,
yo estaré en vuestra sombra, ¡oh hermosamente vivos!

*From *De claro en claro.*

In You I End

This object of love is not an object alone;
it is a beautiful object, and I think that's enough.
Beautiful are her arms, her shoulders, her breasts;
beautiful are her eyes (and how well they lie!).

Desirable, she deceives me, or furtively slips
softly and soft, with sweetness of flesh,
or sinks toward a center more secret than the soul;
or hurts with a fire more real than love.

If I kiss her, I don't speak; if I touch her, I don't believe;
and I grow quiet watching her,
or I sleep in her arms or I die in her spasm,
and in destroying myself I find rest.

Farewell

Perhaps, when I die,
they'll say: "He was a poet."
And the world, forever fair, will shine unconsciously.

Perhaps you won't recall
who I was, but still in you
will sound the anonymous lines that I brought into the world.

Perhaps of me there will remain
nothing, not a single word,
not one of the words for the future that I'm dreaming today.

But seen or unseen,
said or unsaid,
I'll be in your shadow, you who are beautifully alive!

Yo seguiré siguiendo,
yo seguiré muriendo,
seré, no sé bien cómo, parte del gran concierto.

Momentos felices

Cuando lleuve, y reviso mis papeles, y acabo
tirando todo al fuego; poemas incompletos,
pagarés no pagados, cartas de amigos muertos,
fotografías, besos guardados en un libro,
renuncio al peso muerto de mi terco pasado,
soy fúlgido, engrandezco justo en cuanto me niego,
y así atizo las llamas, y salto la fogata,
y apenas si comprendo lo que al hacerlo siento,
¿no es la felicidad lo que me exalta?

Cuando salgo a la calle silbando alegremente
—el pitillo en los labios, el alma disponible—
y les hablo a los niños o me voy con las nubes,
mayo apunta y la brisa lo va todo ensanchando,
las muchachas estrenan sus escotes, sus brazos
desnudos y morenos, sus ojos asombrados,
y ríen ni ellas saben por qué sobreabundando,
salpican la alegría que así tiembla reciente,
¿no es la felicidad lo que se siente?

Cuando llega un amigo, la casa está vacía,
pero mi amada saca jamón, anchoas, queso,
aceitunas, percebes, dos botellas de blanco,
y yo asisto al milagro—sé que todo es fiado—,
y no quiero pensar si podremos pagarlo;
y cuando sin medida bebemos y charlamos,
y el amigo es dichoso, cree que somos dichosos,
y lo somos quizá burlando así la muerte,
¿no es la felicidad lo que trasciende?

Cuando me he despertado, permanezco tendido
con el balcón abierto. Y amanece: las aves
trinan su algarabía pagana lindamente;

*From *El Corazón en su sitio*.

I shall keep on going,
I shall keep on dying,
I shall be part of the great concert, though I'm not sure how.

Happy Moments

When it rains and I go through my files,
and finally burn it all: unfinished poems,
unpaid IOUs, letters from dead friends,
photographs, and kisses kept in a book,
I renounce the dead weight of my obstinate past;
and lucid, I grow large as I give up myself;
and so I poke the fire, and make it blaze,
and hardly know what I feel by this act,
isn't it happiness that exalts me?

When I walk down the street and whistle, carefree
—a cigarette between my lips, my soul ready for the world—
and I speak to the children or go with the clouds,
May pushes in and the breeze opens all,
the young girls show off their naked tanned arms,
their low necklines, their eyes dark with surprise;
and they're overflowing with laughter without knowing why,
splashing a trembling joy everywhere,
isn't it happiness one feels?

When a friend comes to visit, there's nothing in the house,
but my loved one finds olives, anchovies, ham,
cheese, mussels, two bottles of white wine,
and I witness the miracle—knowing what we owe—
and I don't want to think how we'll pay for it all;
and when we drink without stopping and talk and talk,
and the friend is delighted and believes we are too,
and in fact we are, fooling death in this way,
isn't it happiness that transcends?

When I've awakened I stay stretched out on the bed,
with the balcony door open wide to the dawn;
and the birds warble prettily their pagan song;

y debo levantarme, pero no me levanto;
y veo, boca arriba, reflejada en el techo
la ondulación del mar y el iris de su nácar,
y sigo allí tendido, y nada importa nada,
¿no aniquilo así el tiempo? ¿No me salvo del miedo?
¿No es la felicidad lo que amanece?

Cuando voy al mercado, miro los abridores
y, apretando los dientes, las redondas cerezas,
los higos rezumantes, las ciruelas caídas
del árbol de la vida, con pecado sin duda
pues que tanto me tientan. Y pregunto su precio,
regateo, consigo por fin una rebaja,
mas terminado el juego, pago el doble y es poco,
y abre la vendedora sus ojos asombrados,
¿no es la felicidad lo que allí brota?

Cuando puedo decir: el día ha terminado.
Y con el día digo su trajín, su comercio,
la busca del dinero, la lucha de los muertos.
Y cuando así cansado, manchado, llego a casa,
me siento en la penumbra y enchufo el tocadiscos,
y acuden Kachaturian, o Mozart, o Vivaldi,
y la música reina, vuelvo a sentirme limpio,
sencillamente limpio y, pese a todo, indemne,
¿no es la felicidad lo que me envuelve?

Cuando tras dar mil vueltas a mis preocupaciones,
me acuerdo de un amigo, voy a verle, me dice:
"Estaba justamente pensando en ir a verte."
Y hablamos largamente, no de mis sinsabores,
pues él, aunque quisiera, no podría ayudarme,
sino de cómo van las cosas en Jordania,
de un libro de Neruda, de su sastre, del viento,
y al marcharme me siento consolado y tranquilo,
¿no es la felicidad lo que me vence?

Abrir nuestras ventanas; sentir el aire nuevo;
pasar por un camino que huele a madreselvas;
beber con un amigo; charlar o bien callarse;
sentir que el sentimiento de los otros es nuestro;
mirarse en unos ojos que nos miran sin mancha,
¿no es esto ser feliz pese a la muerte?
Vencido y traicionado, ver casi con cinismo

and I know that I ought to get up, but I don't
and I see reflected in the ceiling as I lie on my back
the waves of the sea, the mother-of-pearl rainbow,
and nothing matters to me as I stay there stretched out,
am I not killing time in this way? Escaping fear?
Isn't it happiness that dawns?

When I go to the market I look at the nectarines,
biting my lips not to eat the cherries and the juicy figs,
and the plums that must have fallen from the tree of life,
tempting me so that I think them full of sin.
I ask their price and bargain for a time;
and I get a reduction at last, but then the game's through,
and I pay double the sum—still a small amount—
and the astonished fruit-lady opens wide her eyes,
isn't it happiness that abounds?

When I can say that the day has come to an end,
and with the day its business, its wearying pace,
the race for money, the fight of the dead;
and when so tired and dirty I finally get home,
sit down in the darkened room and put records on,
and Khachaturian or Mozart or Vivaldi appears,
and the music reigns, and again I feel clean,
simply clean and whole, in spite of everything,
isn't it happiness that enfolds me?

When after giving my worries a thousand turns,
I remember a friend, go to see him, and hear,
"I was just this moment thinking of visiting you,"
we talk a long time but not of troubles I have,
since he, much as he'd want to, could not really help;
we speak of Jordan's internal affairs,
of a book of Neruda's, of his tailor, of the wind,
and upon leaving I feel reassured, even calm,
isn't it happiness that conquers me?

To open our windows, to feel the new air;
to walk down a road and smell the honeysuckle bloom;
to drink with a friend; to talk or be still;
to know that the feelings of others are our own;
to see ourselves in the innocent eyes that see us,
isn't this to be happy in spite of death?
Conquered and betrayed, almost cynically to see

75

que no pueden quitarme nada más y que aún vivo.
¿no es la felicidad que no se vende?

El Viejo y el mar
(Glosa a Hemingway)

Erase un hombre viejo.
Fue a pescar y de pronto se encontró con lo innombrable:
la luz con cola impalpable,
la llama fría, la carne
resbalada de la mar fuera de madre.

Erase un hombre viejo,
libre por viejo, quemadamente cano,
que fue a pescar.
Era un hombre
que topó con lo insospechado coleando.

Allí estaba. No podía
creerse, pero estaba provocando lo visible.
Sintió vergüenza y cansancio.
Mas aún luchó. Era un hombre
que se encontró de repente con una gloria posible.

Contó casi sus dedos
al pedirles de uno en uno su esfuerzo de ahora o nunca.
Recogiendo y aguantando se sentía en sus extremos.
Contó el golpe insistente
y mortal en su pecho de cansancio numerado.

Era un hombre. Latía.
Latía contra todo, ferozmente, con rabia.
Se sentía levantado por debajo de sí mismo.
"Ahora o nunca, sostenlo",
le gritaba el hambre grande de su yo sobresaltado.

"Ahora o nunca", rezaba,
maldecía, poniendo
sus uñas erizadas de luz y antigüedad todas en acto.

*From *Rapsodia éuskara.*

that they can't take any more from me, and yet I live,
isn't it happiness that is not for sale?

The Old Man and the Sea
(A Gloss on Hemingway)

There was once an old man.
He went out to fish and then suddenly faced
the unnamable, the light with intangible tail,
the cold flame, the slippery flesh out of the sea,
out of the mother.

There was once an old man,
old and thus free, with hair scorched white,
who went out to fish.
He was a man
who caught the unknown, writhing.

There it was. He was amazed:
he couldn't believe he was making it visible.
He felt apprehensive, weary, shy.
And still he fought. He was a man
who suddenly encountered a possible glory.

He almost counted his fingers as he begged them
now or never to be strong.
And he felt the surge of their effort to the tips.
He counted the insistent and mortal beats,
numbered by weariness, in his breast.

He was a man. He throbbed.
He throbbed fiercely against everything in his rage.
He felt himself lifted from beneath.
"Now or never, hold on, hold on,"
demanded the great hunger of his startled self.

"Now or never," he prayed, or cursed,
asking even his fingernails to work,
roughened as they were by sunlight and age.

Y el físico milagro—sólo físico, puro—
unía heroicamente lo alto con lo bajo.

Era un hombre vulgar: un hombre viejo y terco.
No recuerdo su nombre, pues no fue un dios. Fue sólo
el hombre que uno puede acabar siendo.
Cuando dudaba de todo, la vida le hizo un guiño,
y una trampa, el destino.

¿Qué pasó? Solo un pez. Un pez extraordinario.
Un estúpido hallazgo.
El pez que siglo a siglo persiguieron a muerte
todos los fracasados.
Y allí estaba. Y él dijo: "Ahora o nunca." Fue el acto.

Y sus barbas sudaban, sus ojos trascendían,
sus brazos esforzados aguantaban en alto
la lascivia del mar hecha forma concreta,
la riqueza secreta de los fondos, de pronto
bellamente propuesta.

Era un pez como un hecho. Un hecho extraordinario.
La horrible sacudida de lo arcaico trataba
de no ser, no mostrarse,
y escapaba, burlaba por lo líquido e informe.
Mas él logró que el salto tuviera forma y nombre.

Brillaba el Padre arriba.
Brillaba el mar prado, y encima, un dios insomne.
Y el pescador, cansado, fumaba en holocausto.
No podía pensar. Fumaba lentamente.
Miraba la mar muerta para no ver sus dentros.

Los pájaros salvajes, los voraces rampantes
de los mares mordían el pez que así arrastraba.
Y el pescador fumaba, flotaba en lo indecible,
llevando un esqueleto blanquísimo a remolque.
Erase un hombre viejo. Venció. Y estaba triste.

And the physical miracle—physical alone—
heroically united above and below.

He was an ordinary man: stubborn and old.
I've forgotten his name, as he wasn't a god.
He was only the man we could all finally be.
When he lost faith, life gave him a break,
and destiny a trap.

What happened? Just a fish. An extraordinary fish.
A silly catch, that fish
that all the unsuccessful through the centuries
pursued almost to its death.
And there it was. "Now or never," he said. That was the event.

And his beard sweated, his eyes rolled up,
his strong, strained arms held on as they could
to the sea's lust made concrete form,
the secret wealth of the ocean depths
suddenly beautifully revealed.

The fish was like an event. An extraordinary event.
That horror shaken out of the archaic past
tried not to be, not to be seen,
and it escaped mockingly, in the fluid unformed.
Yet its leap now had form and name.

The Father was shining above.
The stilled sea was shining, and on top a sleepless god.
And the weary fisherman smoked, in a sacrifice.
He smoked slowly. He couldn't think.
He gazed at the dead sea's surface not to glimpse within.

Threatening, voracious, the savage sea birds
devoured the fish he was dragging behind.
The fisherman smoked, and floated on the unutterable,
with the very white skeleton in tow.
There was once an old man. He triumphed. And he was sad.

Sin lengua

Mar de Euskaria, patria abierta,
tú que no tienes fronteras
di en las playas extranjeras,
ola más ola, mi pena.

¡Que nos arrancan la lengua!
¡Que nos roban nuestro canto!
Y hasta mis versos son versos
que traduzco al castellano.

Yo que aprendí a decir "padre",
mas nací diciendo "aitá",
no acierto con el idioma
justo para mi cantar.

He leído a los que mandan.
Me he aprendido mi Cervantes.
Y ahora trato de explotarlos
para salir adelante.

Con mis faltas de sintaxis,
yo, por vasco sin remedio,
pecaré, como Baroja
y Unamuno, de imperfecto.

Porque ellos, aunque me choque,
no supieron escribir.
Doctores tiene mi España
que se lo sabrán decir.

Y si ellos no pudieron,
pese a toda su pasión,
hacer suyo un nuevo idioma,
amigos, ¿qué podré yo?

Abro el alma a cuanto viene.
Busco un mundo sin historia
y un sentimiento de origen
y de dulce desmemoria.

*From *Lo que faltaba*.

Without a Tongue

Borderless fatherland,
Sea of Biscay,
with wave after wave
tell foreign shores of my pain.

That they rip out our tongues!
That they rob us of our song!
And make me translate
even my verses for Spain.

I who learned to say "padre,"
though I said "aitá" when born,[1]
cannot find a language
for singing my song.

I've studied the authorities.
My Cervantes I have read.
And now I try to exploit them
in order to get ahead.

Like Unamuno and Baroja,[2]
imperfect, hopelessly Basque,
I'll sin again and again
with errors in syntax.

For they could not write either—
and I find this really shocking.
My Spain has many professors
who are able to prove it.

And if those writers could not,
however passionate their cry,
make a new language theirs,
then, friends, how can I?

I open my soul to whatever happens.
I seek a world without history,
and a sense of origin,
and the sweet loss of memory.

1. "Aitá" is Basque for "padre," which is Spanish for "father."
2. Miguel de Unamuno and Pío Baroja were well-known writers of Spain's Generation of '98.

Pero hay que hablar, hay que ser,
hay que decirse en la lucha,
y hay que extraer un lenguaje
de lo que sólo murmura.

Yo lo busco. Aquí me expongo
con un dolor que me callo,
furioso como una estrella
y consciente por amargo.

¿Adónde van mis palabras?
¿Adónde mis sentimientos?
¿Para quién hablo, perdido,
perseguido por mis muertos?

¡Mar de Euskaria, rompe en llanto,
y en tu idioma en desbarato,
di, ensanchándote, qué raros
nos sentimos hoy los vascos!

Parábola

Cuando Shanti pensó, lleno de mil razones:
"El patrón debe entenderme", se explicó. Y le expulsaron.
El patrón no entendía de verdad sus razones.
Y Shanti no entendió por qué no le entendía.

Cuando Li-Piao le dijo a Piao-Li: "¿Cómo debo
corregir este texto que llevo al gran examen?",
Piao-Li dijo a Li-Piao: "Si yo fuera tú,
nunca hubiera dudado. Vas a ser rechazado."

Li-Piao cayó en desgracia y Shanti fue expulsado.
Su error fue un mismo error: buscaron lo absoluto.
No hay razones eternas, ni hay verdad objetiva,
ni hay patrón-mandarín sin sentido de clase.

*From *Lo que faltaba*.

But one must talk, keep on going,
and speak up in the fight;
and one must extract a language
from what has been suppressed.

This I seek—and here risk myself,
with a sorrow I do not utter,
with the hot fury of a star,
with consciousness that is bitter.

Where do my words go?
Where go my feelings?
Lost and pursued by my dead,
for whom am I speaking?

Break into tears, Sea of Biscay,
swell up, grow large and say—
in your broken, scattered speech—
how strange Basques feel today!

Parable

When Shanti thought, with his thousand reasons,
"The boss should understand me," he explained himself. And
        they expelled him.
The boss didn't really understand his reasons.
And Shanti didn't understand why his boss did not.

When Li-Piao said to Piao-Li, "How should I
correct this text that I'm taking to the big examination?"
Piao-Li said to Li-Piao, "If I were you,
I would have no doubt. You'll be rejected.

Li-Piao fell out of favor, and Shanti was expelled.
Their mistake was the same: they sought the absolute.
There are no eternal reasons, nor is there objective truth,
nor a mandarin-boss without a sense of class.

La Falsa paz (1)

Peor que la guerra, ¿qué?
¡La paz, la paz!
Esa paz que suena a tiro
y que mata sin alarma.
¡Paz, paz, paz!

*From *Lo que faltaba*.

Informe

Se han estudiado todos los datos del problema.
Se han hecho mil diez fotos. Se han tomado medidas
del lugar del suceso y cuanto le rodea.
Se han aplicado al reo las técnicas modernas,
sin peligro de vida, con médica asistencia.
Después, previo el permiso, se ha machacado el cráneo,
pues algo debe haber que sigue allí secreto.
No se ha encontrado nada que valiera la pena
para hacer racional el supuesto misterio,
aunque se ha recurrido a lo pluscuamperfecto.
Pero no hay criminal que no acabe gritando.
Vamos a examinar a su madre y sus hijos
de un modo humanitario aséptico-anestésico.
Se trata de estudiar, porque es fundamental,
cómo pueden surgir monstruos tan disconformes
como este que estudiamos, no del todo anormal.
Hay que estudiar a fondo a su madre, y salvar
si es posible a sus hijos, operando en directo
esos tiernos cerebros, quizá aún corregibles.
Es una gran empresa superoccidental
que ejercemos en nombre de la Humanidad.

*From *Lo que faltaba*.

False Peace (1)

What's worse than war?
Peace, peace!
That peace that sounds like a shot
and that kills without alarm.
Peace, peace, peace!

Report

All the details of the problem were studied.
A thousand and ten photographs were made.
Measurements were taken of the site of the event and the
    surrounding area.
Modern technology was applied to the prisoner
without endangering his life, with medical assistance.
Then, permission secured, his skull was crushed,
since there must have been some secret still hidden within.
Nothing worthwhile was discovered
to resolve the supposed mystery,
although efforts were made to the nth degree.
But there's no criminal that doesn't end up screaming.
We're going to examine his mother and his children
in an aseptic-anesthetic humanitarian manner.
This will involve the study—fundamental—
of how such nonconforming monsters as this one,
not altogether abnormal, can develop.
One must study thoroughly his mother,
and save his sons if possible, operating live
on those vulnerable brains, perhaps still corrigible.
It is a great super-Western enterprise
that we undertake here in the name of Humanity.

El Misterioso amor

Un beso sólo es un beso.
Dos besos sólo son dos.
A partir del tercero
empieza la confusión,
y si se cierran los ojos
—¿quién eres tú?, ¿quién soy yo?—,
se deslíen las distancias,
se multiplica el amor,
y se rompen los cristales,
y es el sexo un negro sol,
y el cuerpo—tu cuerpo, el mío—,
tras la transverberación,
algo perdido que ahí queda,
y de hecho no soy yo,
ni tú, ni Dios.

*From *Los Espejos transparentes.*

La Puerta

Me he parado, pequeño, ante la enorme puerta
de madera oscura, con bronces historiados.
¿Debo llamar? ¿Debo esperar? ¿Debo algo?
Parece que sí. No sé. Quizá recuerdo
al niño que trataba de llegar a la aldaba.
Yo tampoco llego, de puntillas, ni en sueños.
Y de pronto la puerta se abre lentamente,
despacio, con el leve chirrido de cien siglos,
y muestra ante mí, ansioso, de par en par, cuadrado,
un espejo de plata, y en él, quien no conozco.

*From *Los Espejos transparentes.*

Mysterious Love

A kiss is only a kiss.
Two kisses are only two.
The confusion begins
with the third,
and if you close your eyes
—who are you? who am I?—
the distances dissolve,
love multiplies,
the windows break,
and sex is a black sun,
and the body—yours, mine—
after the penetration,
something lost that remains;
and I am not really I,
nor you, nor God.

The Door

Very small, I have paused before the enormous door
made of dark wood with ornaments of bronze.
Should I knock? Should I wait? Should I do anything?
Probably. I don't know. Perhaps I recall
the child who was trying to reach the door knob.
I can't reach it either, neither on toes nor in dreams.
And suddenly the door swings slowly ajar
with the quiet squeaking of a hundred centuries,
and wide open, it shows me, anxious now,
a square silver mirror, framing someone I don't recognize.

La Máscara

Le dicen a uno: "¡Quítese la careta!"
Uno se la quita, salvando la vergüenza,
pues bien mirado, ¿cómo mostrarse tan desnudo
en este mundo falso de ojos denunciadores?
Mas los guardias son puros, aséptico-anestésicos:
"Sea usted honesto. Quítese la careta."
Me la quito y mi rostro, modelo-modelado,
es tan igual a aquella careta que he tirado,
que los Guardias me dicen más y más irritados:
"¡Quítese la careta! ¡Quítese la careta!"
—"Es mi rostro", les digo. Se ríen. No me creen.
¡Debo de ser tan feo, tan grotesco, increíble!
—"¡Quítese la careta!" Ya no se qué quitarme.
Desgarro mis mejillas, me arranco las pestañas
y algunos funcionarios amables colaboran.
Al fin, tras la careta, las cien caretas tercas,
surge un óvalo liso, sin ojos ni facciones.
Su seguro servidor que firma, aunque no es nadie,
el atestado que ahora le llevará a la cárcel.

*From *Los Espejos transparentes.*

La Cámara octogonal

*(Homenaje a Leonardo
da Vinci)*

Ante un espejo, de frente,
extrañamos al que vemos,
chocamos con el que viene
y está mirando sin vernos.
Si hay otro espejo a la espalda,
sospechando, nos volvemos,
¿y qué decir si aumentamos
más los vértigos del miedo?

*From *Los Espejos transparentes.*

The Mask

They say, "Take off your mask!"
One takes if off, embarrassed,
for how can one stand exposed so naked
in this false world of accusing eyes?
But the cops are aseptic-anesthetically pure:
"Be honest. Take off your mask!"
I take it off, and my model face
is so like the mask I've thrown away
that the Police say again, irritably,
"Take off your mask! Take off your mask!"
"It's my face," I say. They laugh. They don't believe me.
I must be ugly, grotesque, unbelievable!
"Take off your mask!" I don't know what to take off now.
I tear at my cheeks, I yank my eyelashes,
and some obliging officials help out.
Finally, behind the mask, behind a hundred stubborn masks,
appears a smooth oval, with neither eyes nor features.
Yours truly, who signs, although he is nobody,
the accused they will now put in jail.

The Octagonal Chamber

*Homage to Leonardo
Da Vinci*

In front of the mirror we face
we find what we see quite strange;
we collide with the one who approaches
who looks but doesn't see.
If behind us is another mirror,
when we suspect it we turn around;
now what do we say if we increase
this frightening vertigo we've found?

Leonardo imaginó
un octógono de espejos
matemático y estraño.
Quien se ponía en el centro
de ese aparato, y miraba
los incontables reflejos
y las varias perspectivas
de los focos y agua en juego,
terminaba en invisible:
hecho puro desencuentro,
de frente y de espalda se iba
por ocho puertas a un tiempo,
y 8 es el signo de Hermes,
y Hermes, el dios del secreto.
Hubo muchos que jugaron,
sin saber que no era un juego,
al octógono absorbente
del ojo del nuevo insecto.
Y hubo quien nunca volvió
tras de situarse en el centro,
matemático sin duda,
pero lleno de misterio,
que imaginó Leonardo.
Reflejo contra reflejo
se iba desagregando.
¡Gloria a aquel Renacimiento
que, sin magia, consiguió
ciertos cálculos secretos
y un disponer perspectivas
como quien abre misterios!

La Mágica estupidez del tic-tac

Suspendido en el péndulo, esperando,
suspendido en la nada,
en el miedo
de lo que va a pasar,
va a pasar y no pasa . . .

*From *Lírica de cámara*.

90

Leonardo imagined once
a mathematical and very strange
octagonal mirror structure.
Whoever would put himself
in the center of the apparatus
and would look at the countless reflections—
of the foci and water in play—
ended up being invisible;
become pure dis-encounter,
forwards and backwards he'd leave
through eight doors simultaneously;
and 8 is the sign of Hermes,
and Hermes the god of the secret.
Without knowing it wasn't a game,
many came to play
at the absorbing octagon
of the new insect eye.
And there was one who didn't return
after placing himself in the center,
the center Leonardo imagined,
mathematical yet mysterious.
Through the reflections reflecting each other
he split into many and vanished.
Let us praise the Renaissance
that achieved without use of magic
certain secret calculations
and arrangements of perspective—
as one who uncovers mysteries!

The Stupid Magic of the Ticking

Suspended in the pendulum, waiting,
suspended in the nothingness,
in the fear
of what will happen,
what will happen and is not happening . . .

Y el péndulo siguiendo.

Va a pasar y no pasa
nada.
Y ese es el gran terror:
que no pasa nada.

Y el péndulo siguiendo.

Pues todo es esperar, y esperar
que va a pasar algo raro
que no pasa.

¡El miedo!
Ese miedo de esperar lo inesperable.

Y el péndulo siguiendo.

¿Quién ha llamado en la puerta?
¡Nada! ¡Nadie, ni nada!
Pero el péndulo sigue
marcando un compás
como si quisiera cantar o anunciar.

Alfa-1

*Durante su movimiento en la Cámara de Wilson, la partícula ele-
mental ioniza las moléculas de gas que hay en ella, y entonces éstas
se convierten en centros de condensación de gotas macroscópicas
visibles o fotografiables. Este es el principio de la Lírica de
Cámara: Hace posible ver las trayectorias de las partículas elementales aisladas que poseen una carga, o bien, las de los átomos
ionizados*

La instantánea intensidad de lo radiante.
Esta Lírica de Cámara: La Cámara de Wilson
donde, al chocar, se transforman millones de micro-objetos,
y los tantos o los *quantos* como un yo, tan inestables
y veloces que transcurren invisibles.

*From *Lírica de cámara*.

92

And the pendulum swinging.

Something will happen
and nothing is happening.
And that is the horror:
that nothing is happening.

And the pendulum swinging.

Waiting is all, waiting, expecting
that something unusual will happen
that is not happening.

The fear!
That fear of waiting for the unforeseeable.

And the pendulum swinging.

Who has knocked at the door?
Nothing! Nobody, nothing!
But the pendulum keeps swinging,
marking a rhythm
as if it wanted to sing or to speak.

Alpha-1

*During its movement in the Wilson Chamber, the elementary parti-
cle ionizes the gas molecules that are in it, and then they are
converted into centers of condensation of macroscopic drops that
are visible and capable of being photographed. This is the principle
of the Chamber Lyric: It makes it possible to see the trajectories of
the isolated elementary particles that possess a charge, that is,
those of the ionized atoms*

The instant intensity of the radiant,
This Chamber Lyric: The Wilson Chamber
where millions of colliding micro-objects,
and the quantity and the *quanta* like selves, are transformed
with such instability and velocity that they pass unseen.

Esta Lírica de Cámara tan cerrada y más que humana
no es el equivalente de la delicia abstracta
que solía llamarse música de cámara.
Se parece por vacía y por su nada en cascada.
Pero el vacío, hoy en día, es por limpio más sin alma.

Alfa-6

Nada de patetismos. El mesón, pasadas dos millonésimas de se-
gundo, se desintegra en un electrón o un positrón y un neutrino.
Así es mi risa

Si millones de veces por segundo
nace un mundo
en la cámara de Wilson, sin que nadie lo registre;
si proyecto en las galaxias,
pues no es cuestión de tamaño, la magia, el hecho
estúpido, inaudito,
comprendo algo sencillo:
Lo que ocurre
desborda cuanto humanamente pienso.
Y me río de mí mismo.
Y eso es bueno.
Porque esa risa—creo—
es lo que más se parece a un átomo descompuesto.
Y al verso inverso.

*From *Lírica de cámara.*

Delta-3

Lección de Retórica para estudiantes tontamente adelantados, y de
Filosofía fácil para analfabetos inteligentes

Porque el hombre no es humano, y esto hay que irlo
        comprendiendo,

*From *Lírica de cámara.*

This Chamber Lyric beyond humanity and so closed
is not equal to the abstract delight
of what is usually called chamber music.
It resembles it in its emptiness and its flowing nothingness.
But the emptiness, these days, is cleaner without soul.

Alpha-6

No pathos. The meson, two millionths of a second gone by, disinte-
grates into an electron or a positron and a neutrino. That is like my
laughter

If a million times a second
a world is born
in the Wilson Chamber, without anyone recording it;
if I project onto the galaxies—
since it's not a question of size—the magic,
the brute fact, unheard,
I understand something simple:
What happens
goes far beyond whatever I can humanly think.
And I laugh at myself.
And that's fine.
For that laugh—I believe—
is what most resembles a split atom.
And the inverted verse.

Delta-3

Rhetoric lesson for students foolishly advanced, and Philosophy
lesson for intelligent illiterates

Because man is not human, and one must understand this,

porque el hombre fue inventado hace apenas unos siglos,
y va a terminar muy pronto, y nadie habrá que le llore,
pero aún sigue alborotando y afirmando que es quien es
como si no fuera, actuado, más que actuante, el subproducto
de un movimiento más vasto del que apenas es consciente,
y el movimiento sin móvil, no humanista, no moral,
sin una historia que cuente, ni tiempo para contar,
tan variable en apariencia, que hasta se cree en libertad,
uno, ninguno, un millón, sin objetos que le objeten
y así le vuelvan sujeto de su propia realidad,
sin el bonito nosotros en que todos somos uno,
demagógicos, idiotas; sin vergüenza, ni humanismo,
lucha, choca, se transforma, y aún perpetúa los cambios
como un mesón, un Joaquín, un neutrino, un Don Neutrón
que cambian, y no es por gusto, solamente por cambiar.
Lo aburrido es que da igual el más-menos que el bien-mal.
Es la Segunda Ley que nos lleva hacia el cero,
termodinámicamente. Y perdonen, si hablo mal.
Ya sé que los poetas se dan de otro cantar.
Mas yo sé más. Si pudiera, mi verbo sería activo.
No tendría sujeto, ni objeto, ni adjetivos.
Sería impersonal. Sería inexplicable.
Sería un colectivo de sucesos sin nombre:
Un enjambre de cargas; un campo ondulatorio
de frases sin sintaxis vibrando en el vacío.
La nueva poesía que anuncio mas no escribo
porque aún existe el hombre que se cree y que se dice,
y esto es lo que se enseña—Retórica—en las clases
donde los Profesores dictan qué es Poesía.
¿Y para quién escriben hoy día los poetas?
Tan sólo para ellos. Para los estudiantes.
Para que escriban tesis sobre nuestros ejemplos.
Y que perdone el pueblo, nos prestamos al juego.

because man was invented barely a few centuries ago,
and will end very soon, with no one to mourn him,
but he still keeps agitating and affirming that he is who he is
as if, performed upon more than performer, he were not the
    byproduct
of a vaster movement of which he is hardly conscious,
a movement without goal, not humanist, not moral,
without a history that counts, nor time to count,
so changing in its appearance that man almost believes in his
    freedom,
one, none, a million, without objects that could objectify him
and thus turn him subject of his own reality,
without the pretty we in which all of us are one,
demagogues, idiots; without shame or humanism,
he battles, collides, transforms himself, and even perpetuates the
    changes
like a meson, a Joaquín, a neutrino, a Don Neutron
that change, and it is not for fun, only to change.
The bore is that there is no difference between the more-less and
    the good-bad.
It is the Second Law that carries us to zero,
thermodynamically. And pardon me if I speak wrong.
I already know that poets are given to another song.
But I know more. I would make my verb active, if I could.
It would have neither subject, nor object, nor adjectives.
It would be impersonal. It would be inexplicable.
It would be a collective of events without name:
A swarm of charges; an undulating field
of sentences without syntax vibrating in the vacuum.
The new poetry that I announce but do not write
because man still exists who believes in himself and says so:
and this is what is taught—Rhetoric—in the classes
where the Professors dictate what is Poetry.
And for whom do poets write today?
Only for them. For the students.
So they may write their theses on our examples.
And may the people pardon us for lending ourselves to the game.

Empezar, así se empieza, pero di cómo se acaba. ¿Que no hay final?
Bueno. Sólo quería saberlo.

De mis soledades voy.
A mis soledades vuelvo.
Son soledades pobladas
donde mil micro-sujetos,
ignorándose, chocan,
y dan a luz algo nuevo,
se transforman uno en otro,
disparatan el silencio.
No sé quién soy. Nadie es nadie.
Rompo el verbo. Rompo el tiempo
del presente y del futuro.
No hay soledad. No hay sujeto,
ni hay gramática que valga,
ni sintaxis del rodeo,
Ni en la Cámara de Wilson
hay muerte. Sólo un proceso.
Unos cambiamos en otros,
todos en nada. ¡Silencio!
Están matando al fantasma
que me quise tras de muerto,
pero si aún eso me niegan,
me sobran todos los verbos
pasados, pluscuamperfectos,
condicionales, futuros,
en tú, en nosotros, yo o nadie,
¡oh impersonal cero-cielo!

*From *Lírica de cámara.*

Fi-3

*Just starting, that's how one gets started, but tell me how one
finishes. So there's no end? Good. I simply wanted to know.*

From my solitude I go.
To my solitude I return.
It's a populated solitude
where a thousand micro-subjects,
unknowingly collide,
give birth to something new,
into each other are transformed,
render the silence chaos
I know not who I am. No one is anyone.
I break verb. I break time,
present and future.
There is no solitude. No subject,
no worthy grammar,
no subtle syntax,
nor in the Wilson Chamber
is there death. Only process.
Some of us change into others,
all into nothing. In silence!
They are killing the ghost
I wanted for myself after death,
yet even if they deny me that
I have in excess all the verbs
pluperfect, past,
conditional, future,
in you, in us, myself or no one,
impersonal zero-sky!

Fi-4

La nueva poesía debe ser neutra, y a ser posible estúpida. Intento conseguir eso. ¡Pero es tan difícil desprenderse de la manía humanista!

No ha muerto el hombre.
Tan solo una imagen:
La del hombre humano
que se creía alguien.
Puesto que ya ha acabado
canto serenamente:
Tranquilamente expongo
palabras de Don Nadie
sin gritar los dolores
del que sé que no existe.
Y puedo, en consecuencia,
combinar mis palabras
de un modo inexpresivo,
sistemático, neutro.
Puedo, como se dice,
volver a ser correcto,
y en fin, si es necesario,
escribir un soneto.
Pero . . .

*From *Lírica de cámara.*

Mu-6

Con tanto pensar, con tanta moral, con tanta mentira de idear e idear, olvidamos lo serio y más que humano-subjetivo: Lo simplemente verbal

Juego verbal.
Manejamos las palabras para hacerlas chocar,
para hacerlas ser sonido
y no pensar.

Fi-4

The new poetry should be neutral, and possibly stupid. I am trying to achieve that. But it is so difficult to extricate oneself from humanist madness!

Man has not died.
Only an image.
That of human man
who thought himself someone.
Since that image has gone
I can sing in peace:
Calmly I shall speak
the words of Sir No One,
without crying for
him who exists not.
I can thus
combine my words
in an inexpressive mode,
a systematic, neutral mode.
I can always, as they say,
be correct once more,
and if necessary in the end
write a sonnet.
But . . .

MU-6

With so much thinking, with so much moralizing, with so much lying in devising ideas, we forget what is serious and beyond human subjectivity: the simply verbal.

Verbal game.
We manipulate words to make them collide,
to make them sound,
and not to think.

Al fin ellas dicen más
que todas nuestras ideas de lento desarrollo.
Dicen menos, dicen más,
dicen jóvenes y cojas
un cantar,
con la alegría del baile
que viene y va,
con la sabiduría de un viejo renquear,
y un verso de pie quebrado,
que yo no sé todavía, que será.
Y a bailar con e-i-a
lo que no cabe pensar ca-pen-a.
¡Palabras, sólo palabras, sabio ruido verbal!
Pues ya dijo quien lo dijo:
Lo que sea sonará.

Nu-1

*Todo lo que empieza en juego, acaba en sistema. Toda ley oculta una
arbitrariedad. El lenguaje no es una excepción, y romperlo es pre-
cisamente cantar.*

Desintegrar las palabras como el átomo cerrado.
Recombinar sonidos, o sílabas, o breves
partículas en un nuevo sistema.
Conservar el rastro
de ecos y asociaciones meramente sonoras
en la cuartilla-pantalla blanco-pasmada.
Hallar el nuevo sentido
de un gastado sonido.
Y ver lo que no vimos sin ruptura
como la luz idiota de lo brusco-inmediato,
sólo por interrumpida.
Invertir las sílabas.
Repetir y repetir unos mismos fonemas
hasta que equivocando lo sabido
digamos algo imprevisto
que va, y luego
descubriremos lleno de infinitos sentidos.

*From *Lírica de cámara.*

In the end they speak more
than all our ideas slowly born.
They speak less, they speak more,
they speak youth; and you seize
a song,
with the gaiety of the dance
that comes and goes,
with the wisdom of an old limp,
and a broken footed verse,
that I don't yet know, that will be.
And to dance with an ay-ee-ee
what doesn't fit into thought.
Words, only words, wise verbal noise!
For he who said it has already said:
What will be will sound.

Nu-1

*All that begins in play ends in system. Every law hides an arbitrari-
ness. Language is no exception, and to break it is precisely to sing.*

To disintegrate words like an atom.
Recombine sounds, or syllables, or brief
particles into a new system.
Conserve the trace
of merely sonorous echoes and associations
on the astonished white paper sheet.
To find the new sense
of a sound already spent.
And see what without the rupture
we didn't see, the crazy light
of the suddenly immediate.
To turn the syllables around.
Repeat and repeat the same phonemes
till mistaking what we know
we say something unforeseen
that works, and then
we find it full of infinite significance.

Do-senti-do, de-no-de, denodado.
Lo dado. Y el dado
tirado.

Omega-7

*La primavera es una asignatura tan deliciosamente idiota que para
mí siempre acaba en un razonable suspenso.*

Todo está suspendido;
La flor del cerezo, la flor del almendro,
tus ojos que me miran y no veo,
los ojos con que te miro
en la flor del cerezo, en la flor del almendro,
suspenso.
Todo está queriendo ser una brusca realidad,
un susto primaveral.
Todo parece que
va a ser a toda luz instantáneo y material.
Pero, ¿a qué luz? ¿En qué reino?
En el superficial de la naturaleza,
de la literatura,
del hombre y su supuesto sistema de conciencia.
En realidad,
los hechos son otros, atómicos, feroces.
Hay millones de mesones que mueren en un segundo.
Hay protones tan estables
que parecen eternos señorones.
Hay minúsculos estados de materia que perduran
y explosiones más bonitas que las que llamamos flores.
Hay un mundo
donde hablar del amor sólo da risa,
donde hablar de la guerra
irisa,
donde tus ojos son sólo velocidad, destrucción,
aunque tontos me miran
y me admiran admirándose a sí mismos de mirarme.
Esa flor del almendro blanco-rosa, ¡tan bonita!,
está formada por miles de galaxias invisibles

*From *Lírica de cámara.*

Sig-ni-fi-cance, in-fi-ni-ty, sig-ni-fi-chance,
The finite. And the chance throw
of the dice.

Omega-7

*Spring is a course so delightfully idiotic that I always end up being
suspended.*

Everything is suspended.
The blossom of the cherry tree, the blossom of the almond tree,
your eyes that look at me that I don't see,
the eyes with which I look at you
in the blossom of the cherry tree, the blossom of the almond tree,
suspended.
Everything wants to be brute reality,
a springtime shock.
Everything seems about to be
in full light material and momentary.
But in what light? In what reign?
On the surface of nature,
of literature,
of man and his presumed system of consciousness.
In reality,
the facts are different, fierce and atomic.
There are millions of mesons that die in a second.
There are protons so stable
they're like eternal lords and ladies.
There are minute states of matter that will endure
and explosions more beautiful than those we call flowers.
There is a whole world
where mentioning love brings only laughter,
where mentioning war
brings a rainbow,
where your eyes are but destruction and speed,
though foolishly they look at me
and look up to me looking up to themselves by looking at me.
That pink-white blossom of the pretty almond tree
is made of thousands of invisible galaxies

y explosiones infinitas o muertes inacabadas,
¡porquerías!
El instante que vivimos con delicia
en su explosión recogida,
chiquitita,
es mi vida
objetiva.
Y procuro que no explote con su atómica alegría,
pues el mundo, tú y yo, y todo
se perdería.
¡Amor mío! ¡Primavera! ¡Que nos dure todavía
un poquito la mentira!
Y después como ahora, ¡suspenso, suspenso!
por hacer tantas trampas en el examen severo.

Tau-1

La bonita mentira de cada día no engaña a nadie, pero ayuda a vivir, y exalta. No pido más

Amanece inundando.
Los pájaros cantores
cierran los circuitos eléctricos del día.
¡Es la belleza, es la vida!
La cabeza se enciende como una bombilla
a unos doscientos voltios de normal poesía.
¿Es la belleza? No sé.
Es el mundo habitual de la pereza
donde mis números sirven,
mis distancias miden,
mis ideas cuentan,
no se funde el aparato que en mí versifica.
¿Es la vida?
Sé que hay otra
más real, más escondida, menos mía,
pero ésta es mi alegría, mi mentira,
y los átomos me dejan de momento
que viva en mi fantasía,
es decir, en lo vulgar

*From Lírica de cámara.

and infinite explosions and unfinished deaths—
such foolishness.
The instant we live in delight
in its own explosion,
contained, tiny,
is my
objective life.
And I try to contain its atomic joy, so it won't explode,
since the world, you and I, and everything else
would be lost.
My love! Springtime! May a little lie
still last for us a little longer.
And then as now we'll be suspended,
for playing so many tricks on the final exam.

Tau-1

*The pretty everyday lie doesn't fool anyone, but it helps one live,
and it raises one's spirits. I don't ask for more*

Dawn comes in a flood.
The singing birds
close the electric circuits of the day.
It's beauty, it's life!
The head lights up like a bulb
of some two hundred watts of normal poetry.
Is it beauty? I don't know.
It's the slow normal world
where my numbers work,
my distances can be measured,
my ideas count,
and the verse machine within me doesn't break.
Is it life?
I know that there's another
more real, more hidden, less mine,
but this is my happiness, my lie,
and the atoms let me live
for a moment my fantasy:
in the ordinariness of the day

del día que es tan sólo un cada día
sin más, normal,
fabulosamente real.

Zeta-1

*Todo mi alrededor me extraña. También yo debo parecer raro por
ahí fuera. No pertenezco a ese mundo. Para evitar tropiezos, voy a
pedir un carnet de fantasma, porque de identidad, nada.*

Absoluto en la pureza,
sin duración,
sin respiración,
sin aire ni alrededor,
centro de mí mismo mientras llueve fuera dios,
al margen de cualquier yo,
y del desorden del mundo,
y su vegetación, y su repetición,
extrañamente lejos,
y aún más extrañamente cerca, estoy.

Y el cristalino esplendor
porque dos y dos son cuatro,
y cualquier otro modelo
de combinación
es lo mismo, perdón, salvo las apariencias,
siento el horror, lejos,
del implacable, cierto, terrible exterior.
Porque digo que soy, pero
¿quién me hace el que soy?
¿No será un fantasma
él, lo, ése, todos-nadie, tú
que llamo yo?

Solución: El fantasma es un perro.
(Si es que eso es solución.)

*From *Lírica de cámara*.

that is just an average day
with nothing more—normal,
fabulously real.

Zeta-1

*Everything around me I find strange. I too probably seem peculiar
out there. I don't belong to that world. To avoid any pitfalls, I'm
going to request a ghost card—certainly not an identification card.*

Absolute in purity,
without duration,
without breath,
without environs or air,
center of myself while outside god rains,
at the edge of any "I,"
and of the world's disorder,
and its vegetation, and its repetition,
strangely far away,
and even more strangely near, there I am.

And the crystalline splendor
because two plus two make four,
and any other permutation
is the same, excuse me, except for appearances;
I feel the horror, far away,
of the implacable, certain, terrible external.
Because I say that I am, but
who makes me what I am?
Couldn't the he, it, that one, everyone-no one, you
be a ghost
that I call "I"?

Solution: The ghost is a dog.
(If that's a solution.)

Zeta-2

*He aquí algunas conclus-IONES, de cara a la realidad, y algunas
consideraciones, también IONES, sobre el tiempo que no cuenta y
el YO-NONES del perro.*

Las cosas parecen muertas
aunque en verdad no lo están.
La vida corre por ellas
de soledad en soledad.
Existen el pasado y el futuro,
creo.
Pero no existe un presente mensurable.
Sólo existe el instante que es el tiempo sin tiempo,
el fulminante momento
de lo real en el acto de los fusilamientos,
el hoy al cero:
Yo, perro
saltando y corriendo.

Existen los enjambres colectivos de sucesos:
Yo mismo, creo,
aunque yo no soy un yo, soy sólo el signo
de un sistema de conjuntos
variables y bien dispuestos a lo probable y lo abierto
que pueden manejarse,
funcionalmente seguirse y calcularse
hasta llegar a unas cifras, símbolos, resultados
que al fin tropezarán con ciertas realidades
misteriosas o impensables.
Creo
como creen los perros.

Mas ¿cómo morder el hecho que tratamos
de salvar con pensamiento y santo esfuerzo?
Tras tantas micro-batallas,
yo no aseguro ya nada.
¡Me siento en el furor del átomo, tan poco,
tan loco!
Pero digo lo probable.
Matemático-estadístico, pensando en lo que al fin

*From Lírica de cámara.

110

Zeta-2

*I have here some conclus-IONS, in the face of reality, and some
considerations, also IONS, about time's not counting, and the yap-
ping I-NONS of the dog.*

Things seem dead
though they're really not.
Life runs through
their solitudes.
Future and past exist,
I believe,
but no measurable present.
Only the instant that is time outside time,
the lightning moment
of the real in the executionary act,
today become zero:
I, a dog
jumping and running.

The collective swarms of events exist:
Such as I myself, I believe,
though I am not an I, but just the sign
of a system of connections,
variable and inclined to the probable and the open,
a system managing itself,
calculating,
finally becoming figures, symbols, results,
and then, accidently,
mysterious and unthinkable realities.
I believe
like dogs.

But how do I get a bite on this fact,
which we try to handle with holy energy and thought?
After many micro-battles,
I am sure of nothing now.
In the wild activity of the atom, I feel small
and crazy.
But I'll say what is probable.
Mathematically-statistically, thinking that in the end

solucionará como estable lo que doy por improbable,
yo creo, yo, reo,
que corro, salto y ladro, quiero y no muerdo,
y solamente solo, sentado en mi culo, pienso.

Poesía, Sociedad Anónima

Como yo no soy yo, represento a cualquiera
y le presto mi voz a quien aún no la tenga;
o repito otras voces que siento como mías
aunque, hasta sin querer, siempre de otra manera.

Parezco personal, mas digo lo sabido
por otros hace siglos. O quizás, ayer mismo.
Ojalá me repitan sin recordar quien fui
como ahora yo repito a un anónimo amigo.

¡Oh futuro perfection! No hay otra permanencia
que la de ser un eco corregido por otros
que no sabrán mi nombre, ni—espero—mi aventura.
Tampoco yo sé bien quién habla en mi conciencia.

Si algún día un muchacho nos plagia sin saberlo
y en él, lo ya sabido, vuelve a ser un invento,
estaremos en él, invisibles, reales,
como otros, ahora en mí, son corazón de un ave.

Es eso, y no los versos guardados en los libros,
lo que, venciendo el tiempo, sin forma durará
en la obra colectiva y anónima, aún en ciernes,
transformando y creando conciencia impersonal.

*From *Operaciones poéticas*.

what I find improbable will prove to be stable,
I'll believe, I myself, culprit,
and I run, jump and bark, want to bite and do not,
and alone, sitting on my behind, I think.

Poetry, Inc.

As I am not I, I represent anyone
and offer my voice to him who has not one;
or I repeat other voices that feel like my own
that I change without wanting to another style.

I appear to be personal, but I say what was known
by others centuries past. Or perhaps yesterday.
I hope that others not knowing who I was
repeat me as now I repeat an anonymous friend.

Perfect future! There's no other permanence
than that of an echo corrected by those
who won't know my name or adventure—I hope.
Neither do I know who speaks in my conscience.

If a boy unknowingly plagiarizes us one day
and the already known returns as invention in him,
we shall be in him, invisible, real,
as others now in me are heart of a bird.

It is that, and not the verses kept in the books,
which, conquering time, without form will endure
in the incipient collective work that is anonymous,
transforming and creating impersonal conscience.

La Poesía se me escapa de casa

No seré nunca el que fui,
ni mis versos serán lo que yo quise.
Quizá
alguien me copie mal
para mayor difusión, confusión.
De ese modo, si no de otro,
desapareceré.
¿Pues quién seré, quién será
yo, nosotros, usted, él?
Ni él, ni yo;
seremos sólo una voz
para todos en el limbo de la unión.
¡Que me plagie el que al plagiarme
se equivoque así de yo!
¿Que en él sea yo un amor
sin distinción,
y también, aunque no cuente,
un dolor
como él en mí, quién, qué, ¡oh!

*From *Operaciones poéticas*.

La Poesía se besa con todos

Recordar mal
que es como se recuerdan los poemas de verdad,
confundir y cambiar
es participar, re-crear   .
y vivir como propia la obra que el poeta
creía que era suya pero sacó a la calle
tan guapa, provocativa, tan joven y descarada
que todos la redecían
y contaban a su modo cómo era
una noche con ella.

Todo poema si vale se transforma en otros labios,

*From *Operaciones poéticas*.

My Poetry Runs Away from Home

I shall never be the one I was,
nor my verses what I wanted them to be.
Perhaps
someone may miscopy me
for greater diffusion, confusion.
In that way, if not another,
I'll disappear.
Then who will I be, who will be
I, we, you, he?
Neither he nor I;
we'll be only a voice
for all in the limbo of the union.
May whoever mistakes my "I"
go ahead and plagiarize me!
That in him I may be a love
without distinction,
and, though it doesn't count,
a sorrow too,
like him in me, who, what, oh!

The Poem Kisses Everyone

To remember poorly,
the way one remembers true poems,
to confuse and change them
is to share, re-create,
and live as one's own the poem the poet
thought was his when he took her out on the street,
so beautiful, provocative, young and sassy
that everyone spoke her again and again,
describing, each in his own way,
a night spent with her.

Every worthy poem is transformed on others' lips,

y sólo así, equivocado, vuelve a ser un amor
nuevo y veloz.
El poeta que un día lo sacó a pasear
sólo es uno entre otros muchos
y quizá no el mejor
de cuantos, entre chismes y feliz mala memoria,
recuerdan el amor de esa canción
que cambia de forma
y putita, me digo: ¿Quién creó?
Pues es diferente según quién la besa
y es para cualquiera, el único amor.

Las Máscaras
(Función de Uno hacia Ene)

No, nunca se está solo.
                    Me adivino en los otros
pues cuanto más me oculto,
                    más me parezco a todos.
Soy una multitud.
                    No estoy solo aunque pienso.
Represento a cualquiera
                    y al yo en que a veces creo.
Soy sólo un comediante
                    perdido en sus papeles.
Mis máscaras ocultan
                    que yo no tengo rostro.
Los unos somos otros
                    y todos juntos, nadie.
Porque los hombres tienen
                    vocación de fantasmas.
No quiero limitarme.
                    Juego a las apariencias.
Cuando digo no digo,
                    alquilo mi vacío.
Simulo realidades
                    pues yo en rigor no existo.
Me descubro en los otros
                    y los otros son uno.

*From *Función de uno, equis, ene.*

and only by being mistaken does she return
as a new and sudden love.
The poet who one day took her for a walk
is but one among many
and perhaps not the best
of those who, amid gossip and felicitously bad memory,
remember the love in that song
that changes form,
a little whore, I say: Who created her?
For she is different for everyone who kisses her,
and for anyone the one and only love.

Masks
(Function of One to the Nth)

No, one's never alone.
               In others I find myself,
since the more I hide,
                    the more I'm like everyone else.
I am a multitude,
               Whatever I think, I'm not alone.
I represent anyone
                  including the me in which I sometimes
      believe.
I'm but a comedian
               lost in his roles.
My masks hide the fact
               that I don't have a face.
We are each other
             and all together no one.
For human beings have
              the calling of ghosts.
I don't want limits.
            I play at appearances.
When I speak I don't speak,
                I rent my emptiness.
I simulate realities
            since I don't really exist.
I discover myself in others
             and the others are all one.

Perdidos entre espejos
              sin fondo, ¿quiénes somos?
Bajo nuestros disfraces
              se oculta lo invisible.
¿Dónde estamos? ¿Qué pasa?
                    transparencia sin rostro.
Si todos somos uno,
              nadie es nadie, amor mío.
No podemos amarnos.
              Somos todos el mismo.
Al querer a los otros
              sólo adoro mi imagen.
La soledad no existe.
                    ¿Quién estuviera solo?
Soledad impensable.
              Lo absoluto no habla.
¿Qué sentiría un hombre
              de verdad solitario?
Los números enteros
              son meras abstracciones.
¿Qué soy salvo un continuo
                    sin hondura posible?
Sólo soy un enjambre
              de posibles variantes.
Nunca me reconozco
              ni recuerdo de veras.
Un hombre solitario
              sería un dios, no un hombre.

La Lata (de vivir)

"Los seres que viven aquí abajo piensan que Dios está en lo alto,
pero los ángeles en el cielo, dicen que Dios está en la tierra."
                                        —Sepher-Al-Zohar.

Abre y vacía una lata.
Mete dentro el abrelatas.
Cierra después la lata soldándola bien
y la esconde donde no pueda encontrarse.

  *From *La Higa de Arbigorriya.*

Lost in backless mirrors
          who are we?
Beneath our disguises
          the invisible hides.
Where are we? What's happening?
          faceless transparency.
If we are one, love,
          then no one is anyone.
We can't love each other.
          We are all the same.
When I love others
          I love only my image.
Solitude doesn't exist.
          Who could be alone?
Unthinkable solitude.
          The absolute doesn't speak.
What would a truly
          solitary man feel?
Whole numbers
          are mere abstractions.
What am I
          but a shallow continuum?
I'm only a swarm
          of possible variants.
I never recognize myself
          nor remember correctly.
A solitary man
          would be a god, not a man.

The Can (of Living)

"The beings who live down here think that God is above, but the angels in the sky say that God is on earth."
          —Sepher-Al-Zohar

He opens and empties a can.
He puts the can opener inside.
Then he closes the can, soldering it well,
and hides it where it cannot be found.

Luego sube a un barco,
y se va.
Va a buscar el abrelatas que él ha escondido en la lata,
en la lata que ha escondido tirándola al mar,
pues piensa, trascendental:
"¿Para qué serviría un abrelatas
que no fuera difícil de encontrar?"

Esa es la lata, la lata
que es imposible evitar:
la lata del abrelatas
que está dentro de la lata
que sin él no se puede ya rajar.
La lata de la existencia
que nos gusta complicar
por el vicio del misterio,
por el vicio del secreto,
porque nos cuesta creer
que el acá es más que el allá.

La Materia

A veces la materia se dice a sí misma.
¿Qué hacen los formadores cuando creen configurarla?
Nada.
La materia les domina y ellos hacen lo que dicta su presencia.
Porque formarla es amarla, levemente acariciarla
con manos temblorosas
y dejar al fin que se haga sólo lo que ella quería
según un secreto propio que ahora proyecta hacia fuera.
Pues es ella quien se mueve
cuando parece—¡ironía!—que es el hombre quien crea.

*From *Poemas prometeicos*.

Later he gets on a boat
and leaves.
He will search for the can opener he's hidden in the can,
in the can he's hidden by tossing it in the sea,
thinking, transcendentally:
"What good is a can opener
that is not hard to find?"

That's the can—the problem—
that's impossible to avoid:
the problem of the can opener
that is in the can
that without it cannot be opened.
The problem of existence,
that we like to complicate
by our weakness for mystery,
by our weakness for secrets,
because it's hard to believe
that the here and now is more than the beyond.

Matter

Matter speaks at times.
What do the shapers do who think they give it form?
Not a thing.
The matter governs them, and its presence dictates what they do.
For to shape it is to love it, to caress it lightly
with hands that are trembling,
and to let it do as it likes in the end
according to its secret now making itself known.
Thus, ironically, it is matter that moves
when it seems that it is man who makes!

Puntualización

Cuando una escultura se ve desde fuera,
no se ve nada, porque es sólo apariencia.
Lo que hay que ver es qué la rodea;
no lo que ella es, ser-sería sumergida,
sino aquello que ella logra
fuera de sí, que sea.

¿Y qué es entonces lo que es?
La milagrosa evidencia
que esa escultura centra, mas no es,
lo que ella crea y proyecta
furiosamente hacia fuera, mas no es,
escupiendo exultante su evidencia
con su central rabia-idea,
con su normal indecencia,
musgo, lluvia y lo que sea,
queriendo ser lo que no,
                              nunca es.

*From *Poemas prometeicos.*

Dando forma

Energía concentrada. Disparo retenido.
Hasta que un martillazo
pone en forma la estrella de los gritos.

Y brilla, mas sólo brilla porque en torno hay un vacío,
hueco inmenso,
espacio para el posible ser que nos muestra el silencio.

El hombre, sí, es prometeico,
entre la rabia y el fuego,
y entre el yunque, y entre el grito, y entre el hierro, y entre el
     miedo.

*From *Poemas prometeicos.*

Specification

When one sees a sculpture from outside,
as it is only appearance, one sees nothing.
What one sees is what surrounds it,
not what it is, a submerged would-be,
but what it gains
from outside itself, that it becomes.

And what is it then?
The miraculous visibility
which the sculpture centers, but is not,
which it creates and furiously projects
outward, but is not,
throwing out jubilantly its visibility
in its central idea-madness,
in its normal indecency,
moss, rain, and whatever,
wanting to be what it never,
                          ever is.

Giving Form

Concentrated energy. A gunshot held back.
Till the hammer stroke gives form
to the cries' star.

And it shines, but only for being in a void,
an immense hollow,
space for the possible being who shows us silence.

Yes, man is Promethean,
amid rage and fire,
anvil, cry, iron, and fear.

123

Creando, y más, más creciendo: Dando forma a lo imposible
y al espacio
que quisiera ser la nada, devorarnos, anularnos.

No hay más

Fuera está lo de dentro,
     visible, exacto.
Dentro, no hay nada
     (¿o hay sobresalto?).
Fuera, compacto,
     toco lo dado.
Dentro, ¿un temblor?
     No hay que nombrarlo
pues fue vencido,
     resuelto en tacto,
más que querido,
     más que pensado.

Ciertos secretos
     hay que callarlos
por dignidad,
     porque uno es vasco.

*From *Poemas prometeicos.*

El Boquete

Hay un centro perforante
     que se abre y más se abre.
Hay un espacio vacío
     que nos devora, anhelante.
¿Y si ese fuera el misterio
     al que llamamos silencio?
¿Y si el final de las formas
     fuera sólo un agujero?

*From *Poemas prometeicos.*

Creating, then growing: Giving form to the impossible
and to space,
that would be nothingness, that would devour us, annihilate us.

There's No More

Outside is what is inside,
      visible, exact.
Inside there is nothing
      (or is there fright?).
Outside, compact,
      I touch the given.
Inside, a tremor?
      It must not be named
for it was defeated,
      tactfully resolved,
more than wanted,
      more than thought.

Certain secrets
      must be kept silent
for dignity,
      for being Basque.

The Gap

There is a center with a hole
      that widens more and more.
There is an empty space
      that devours us eagerly.
And if that were the mystery
      that we call silence?
And if the end of all forms
      were only a hole?

Sólo el pensarlo da miedo.
　　Da cero.

Lo Neutro

A veces, cuando me pierdo,
siento una cosa rara. Digamos: la belleza.
¿Belleza? Palabra vana.
Digamos, no belleza, digamos le indiferencia
con que se admite todo.
Digamos, la aceptación que lo vuelve todo hermoso.
Digamos cómo la risa se funde con el sollozo.
Digamos cómo lo chico y lo grandioso es lo mismo
y cuánto cuentan las olas que al romperse no hacen ruido.
No es el amor. Es la paz
neutral del ritmo del mundo:
la dulce luz de lo nulo.

*From *Buenos días, buenas noches.*

Paz cósmica

Cuando rompe la mar
y uno escucha largamente, y escucha sin pensar,
dejándose llevar,
la procesión de los mundos que vienen y que van,
el rumor adivinado de las olas en las playas
que no sé dónde están
la sucesión absoluta,
la continuidad,
donde los gritos aislados alzan un absoluto
pretendiendo heroicidad,
y se sabe que esos gestos no significan nada,
y la igualdad
que firman barriendo las olas de la mar
cuenta más que las proclamas de los hombres,

*From *Buenos días, buenas noches.*

and absorbing their laws,
it dictates a cosmic peace
beyond:
A cosmic peace.
A cosmic
peace.
Then . . .

Saintly Idiocy

There's no future.
Whatever we try
is never concluded.
Promethean humanists, Christians, Marxists,
you are all mad. Don't you see?
We're truly neither going nor coming nor moving along.
We're in a nothingness: how do we get out?
If only contrition or revolution
were useful, But they're not. So?
We're all saints.
We're all Marxists, Christians, idiots
and disgraceful fools!

Peace opens wide its arms
to be executed thoughtlessly.
Why, and with what, and in the name
of what should I still fight?
All has suddenly lost its nominal dress
to become real,
real,
truly furious,
purely efficient,
beautiful and happy, as idiotic
as saintliness!

Vuelve al acá

La alegría imparcial.
La dicha indiferente.
La vida como viene
sin más.

        Todos vamos navegando. Todos hemos trabajado.
        Todos hemos luchado creyendo en un final.
        ¡Qué final! El de aquel vals
        de las olas que vienen y van.

Y el azul, siempre allí lejos,
era bello, tan, tan bello
como si girara al cero
sin acabar.

        Pobres hombres prometeicos que tratáis
        de transformar el mundo, y aún creeis
        en la técnica, el trabajo y la velocidad.
        No salís del más aca.

El más allá, ¿no está aquí?
¿Y la felicidad
no consiste en renunciar?
Ven acá, más, más aca.

*From *Buenos días, buenas noches.*

Total, cero

La explosión de la alegría,
la locura del día a toda luz,
la risa irracional . . .
Y pensar
que en este mismo momento
miles y miles de estrellas se están desintegrando
allí, lejos:

*From *Buenos días, buenas noches.*

Return to the Near

Impartial cheer.
Indifferent joy.
Life as it comes
without more.

    We all go navigating. We have all worked.
    Believing in an end we have all fought.
    What end! The one of that waltz
    of the waves that come and go.

And the blue, always there in the distance,
was beautiful, as beautiful
as if it rotated in a zero
without stop.

    Poor Promethean men who try
    to transform the world, and still believe
    in technology, work, and speed.
    You won't leave the near.

The beyond, isn't it here?
And doesn't happiness
consist in renouncing?
Come near, much, much nearer.

Total, Zero

The explosion of joy,
the madness of the day in full light,
the irrational laugh . . .
And to think
that in this very moment
thousands and thousands of stars disintegrate
there, far away:

¡y ay rabiar!
que donde no pensamos ni podemos pensar
miles, y miles, y miles de atomos se entrechocan,
se transforman, se disparan
y alteran sus micromundos
como si el sol de repente viviera en uno mil siglos.

Y pensar
que uno va, y luego se enfada
con su chica por diez, doce,
tres coma catorce dieciséis minutos de retraso
a la hora de la cita.
¡Qué tontería enfadarse!
¡Qué tontería llorar!
¡Qué tontería dejar de besarse y más besarse
cuando en cada instante revienta total
una noche estelar!

Como el átomo

Nos asesinamos (por amor, ¡claro!)
pensando en qué feliz será la humanidad
cuando hayamos acabado de matar.
Hay que disculparnos.
Vivimos en pleno crimen pasional.

Entrechocamos y a veces hasta nos hacemos daño
sin querer.
Y nos transformamos
en otros, sin saber
quién es el otro, pero saludando:
Buenos días. Buenas tardes. Perdone usted.

Si los átomos hablaran dirían igual
cuando revientan a ciegas o se desintegran,
viven en un campo donde no existen sueltas
unidades concretas.
La indiferencia es entonces
un mecánico perdón que se dispersa.

*From *Buenos días, buenas noches.*

132

And, oh, to rage!
that where we neither think nor can think
thousands and thousands and thousands of atoms collide,
transforming themselves, shooting out,
and altering their microworlds,
as if the sun suddenly lived in one thousand centuries.

And to think
that one goes, and then gets angry
with his girlfriend for ten, twelve,
three comma fourteen, sixteen minutes for being late
for the time of the date.
How foolish to get angry!
How foolish to cry!
How foolish not to kiss and kiss again
when in each instant
a stellar night totally explodes!

Like the Atom

We assassinate ourselves (for love, of course)
thinking how happy man will be
when we
no longer kill.
We must be forgiven.
We live in criminal passion.

We collide and hurt ourselves
without intending.
And we transform ourselves
into others, without knowing
who the other is, but greeting:
Good morning. Good evening. Pardon me.

If atoms could speak, they would utter the same
whether they blindly explode or decay;
they live in a field where concrete wholes
do not exist.
Sameness is thus
a mechanical pardon dispersed.

133

La Brisa

Cuando parece que nada significa ya nada,
nos queda una alegría:
La falta de sentido:
                    la brisa.
Todo parece suelto y es sin ser:
Vibra.
Se parece en lo absoluto a una dicha no dicha,
llega al límite del hombre
mortal de cada día,
y rompiendo sus fronteras nos descubre que podemos
ser otras criaturas, tener otras razones,
reinventar la vida.

¡Transparencia de la brisa,
campo sin centros concretos,
onda del mundo en que todos vamos desapareciendo,
vestidos de blanco, con sombrero de paja,
y, ligeros, sonriendo!

*From *Buenos días, buenas noches.*

La Falsa paz (2)

Los átomos establecen un sistema;
los hombres, otro,
y parece que dominan el tumulto de los micros
que se entrechocan, cambian, no duran ni un adiós
pues en rigor no están en ningún lado nunca.

La luz que nos parece tranquilamente tonta
oculta una miríada de furias y locuras,
de muertes sin tragedia
y de revoluciones
que, por rápidas, se olvidan enseguida.

Lo nuestro va más lento. Tan lento como un verso.

*From *Buenos días, buenas noches.*

The Breeze

When it seems that nothing means anything any more,
one pleasure remains for us:
Nonsense:
            the breeze.
Everything seems disconnected, unreal.
Vibrating.
Resembling in the absolute an unspoken joy,
reaching the limits of mortal man
each day
and breaking his frontiers to show us that we could
be other creatures, have other reasons,
reinvent life.

Transparent breeze,
field without concrete centers,
wave of the world in which we are all disappearing,
dressed in white, with straw hat,
and, carelessly, smiling.

False Peace (2)

Atoms establish one system;
men, another;
and the tumult of the particles seems to dominate,
the particles that collide, change, don't last a goodby,
existing nowhere.

The tranquil light apparently mindless
hides manifold anger and madness,
untragic deaths
and revolutions, at once forgotten for their suddenness.

Ours goes more slowly. As slowly as a verse.

La Posesión (2)

¡Oh inmensidad!, nada hay dentro de tus multiplicaciones
salvo yo que no soy yo sino tan sólo el sujeto
de ese lenguaje que suele decirse que es humano.
Se pronuncia lo impensable, se calcula lo increíble,
nos parece de repente que somos dominantes
cuando somos lo sujeto por el objeto clamante
que no, no, no cabe nunca dentro de nuestras ideas
sólo vociferantes. Somos la voz de nadie.
No somos nunca nosotros sino lo otro en nosotros
poseídos por la nada del nadie delirante.

*From *Buenos días, buenas noches.*

La Gramática

Pretéritos imperfectos, futuros perfectos
estáis llenos de versos.
Después de tanto lirismo, yo, gramático, pienso
en cuanto reina latente,
y en lo intenso y aún no extenso,
y en lo que a veces sólo
parece combinatorio, sonambúlico e indefenso.
Pienso
cruelmente contra mí lo que no debo,
ferozmente repleto de misterios.
Y juego.

Sé que al fin la mecánica del verso y la sintaxis
dirán lo que no quiero.
Juego.
No al inconsciente, sólo según el reglamento.
Y no hay musa, ni dios, y por eso
tengo miedo.
Pero maquinalmente, juego.
La Gramática es mi reino
y dios o la musa, cero.

*From *Buenos días, buenas noches.*

136

Possession (2)

Oh immensity! Within your multiplications there is
only I, that am not I but rather just the subject
of that language that is usually called human.
The unthinkable is pronounced, the incredible is calculated,
it suddenly appears to us that we are dominant
when we are subject to the object clamoring
that it does not, not ever, fit within our ideas
vociferous only. We are the voice of no one.
We are never we but rather that other in us
possessed by the nothingness of the delirious no one.

Grammar

Past imperfects, future perfects,
you are full of verses.
After so much lyricism, I, grammatical, think
about what governs unseen
and what is contained within, not yet revealed,
and what at times can seem
only combinatory, somnambulatory, without defense.
I think
thoughts against myself that I should not,
fiercely mysterious as I am.
And I play.

I know that finally the mechanics of syntax and verse
will say what I don't want to say.
I play.
Not to the unconscious, but according to the rules.
And there is no god, nor muse,
and so I am afraid.
But mechanically I play.
Grammar is my kingdom
and god or the muse, zero.

El mundo surgirá cuando organice
el animal, celeste y adorable palabreo.

Insectos

Calor blanco de estío. Y un enjambre resonante
de mínimos que chocan sin conciencia,
se transforman uno en otro, se confunden,
y más allá de la unidad centrada
hierven efervescentes, y se pierden.

Tarde tórrida de Agosto poblada por la ausencia
de los múltiples inquietos, rumorosos
que son pero no son. ¡Ay, sin embargo
esa vida feroz, sin centro, sigue!
Es un vuelo nupcial hacia la muerte.

El hombre fue barrido hace ya tiempo.
Ahora presenciamos la muerte del insecto.
Y un éxtasis total y destructivo
permite descubrir, eco en lo hueco,
la belleza vacía: El ¡oh! del cero.

*From *Buenos días, buenas noches.*

Terror de lo abierto

Laberinto de fuera,
       figuras, rodeos;
laberinto de dentro,
       focos, espejos.
¿Qué se descubre?
       El espacio sin centro,
la conciencia sin nadie
       y el mundo al cero.
No hay vigilante.

*From *Buenos días, buenas noches.*

The world will emerge when the animal,
celestial and adorable wordsmith, makes order.

Insects

White heat of summer. And a buzzing swarm
of minima colliding without consciousness
one into another transformed:
beyond the teeming centered whole
they seethe and disperse and disappear.

Torrid afternoon in August
covered by the absence of the unquiet multiples
that are but are not. Nonetheless
that ferocious uncentered life goes on!
It's a nuptial flight toward death.

Man was swept away some time ago.
Now we witness the insect's death.
And a total, destructive ecstasy
allows, as an echo in the void,
the empty beauty to appear: the zero.

Terror of the Open

Labyrinth without,
        figures, circles;
labyrinth within,
        foci, mirrors.
What does one find?
        Space without center,
consciousness without man,
        the world at zero.
There is no guard,

139

No hay nadie en medio.
¡Terror! Es el espacio
    simplemente abierto.
Se grita. Y es terrible,
    no hay eco.
Y uno vuelve a la cueva
    y al miedo,
y a hablar consigo mismo
    del cero-cielo.
Laberinto final: Serpiente
    del pensamiento.

Aquí está el allí

A veces uno piensa que no piensa
¡y es tan feliz entonces que hasta piensa
que las cosas no piensan porque callan
y que son dichosas, o dichas sin palabras ociosas!
Y así otra vez se equivocan las inmensas distancias
que existen entre los hombres y ese mundo
neutro, animal, divino, o ¿cómo llamarlo?,
que existe fuera nuestro sin conciencia propia.
Fuera o dentro, ¿qué quiere decir esto? Sólo el hombre lo sabe.

¡Distancias vertiginosas! Aquí, el hombre; allí, las cosas.
O allí, el hombre que huye y huye
de la común existencia en que el objeto se asienta.
El ojo y el pensamiento nos alejan de las manos
fabriles y cariñosas que buscan firmes contactos.
El ojo y el pensamiento sólo fabrican fantasmas.
Son las burlas que los dioses materiales
les plantean a los hombres tonto-trascendentales.
Pero el más allá está aquí. Y eso el hombre lo sabe.

*From *Poemas órficos.*

no one in the middle.
Terror—of the space
    that is simply open.
One cries out. It's terrible:
    there is no echo.
And one returns to the cave,
    and to the feeling of fear,
to talk to oneself
    of the zero-sky.
The final labyrinth:
    the serpent of thought.

The Beyond is Here

At times one thinks that he doesn't think
and is then so happy that he even thinks
that things don't think because they are still
and content, or lucky not to have idle words!
And thus one mistakes the great distances again
that exist between men and that neutral world,
animal, divine, or—what would you say?—
that without consciousness exist outside ourselves.
Outside or inside, what does this mean? Only man knows.

Dizzying distances! Here man; there, things.
Or there, man who flees and flees
the existence he has in common with the object.
Eye and thought separate us from hands,
hard-working and caring, that seek firm hold.
Eye and thought make only ghosts.
These are the jokes the material gods
play on men, transcendental fools.
But the beyond is here. And that man knows.

¿Qué es esto que recuerdo?

La vida, a los poetas, suele hacerles confidencias
que algunas veces recuerdan.
Por eso escriben versos que no entienden, si piensan,
pero saben que son ciertos, y en lo oscuro les hablan
de una patria lejana y una matria sin alma.

*From *Poemas órficos.*

Las Metamorfosis

Esa pulsión del Eros que en mí levanta al hombre
podría levantar a un dios o a un toro,
o a un laurel, o también a una lluvia de oro.
Así dicen las fábulas, y es cierto,
tan fácilmente cambiantes vivimos uno en otro
como esas nubes que nunca tuvieron nombre propio.
Lo instantáneo es lo absoluto. Las metamorfosis,
los disfraces del oculto que vive haciéndonos trampas,
o que quizá no vive, solamente aparenta
como si eso le sirviera de consuelo.

*From *Poemas órficos.*

Volveremos. Y entonces . . .

Volveremos a nacer, y seremos,
no lo que fuimos, ni lo que pensamos,
sino aquello que a veces presentimos.

Volveremos, y no nos llamaremos
como ahora nos llamamos todavía
pese al trueno del dios que nos habita.

*From *Poemas órficos.*

What Is This I Recall?

Life sometimes confides in poets
secrets they occasionally recall.
So they write verses they know to be true but don't understand,
and those verses speak to them in the dark
of a fatherland far away and a motherland without soul.

Metamorphoses

That impulse of Eros that in me lifts up man
could lift a god or a bull,
a laurel, or shower of gold.
Thus say the myths, and it's true;
so easily changing from one into another
do we live like those clouds that never had their own name.
The instantaneous is the absolute. The metamorphoses,
disguises of him hidden within who lives
to trick us, or perhaps does not live,
but only pretends, as if that were comfort enough.

We Shall Return. And Then . . .

We shall be born again, and then we'll be
not what we were, nor what we thought,
but what at times we foreboded.

We shall return, and we won't be called
what because of the thunder of the god within us
we still call ourselves now.

Volveremos. Tan distintos
del que somos, que quizá no recordemos
quiénes fuimos o somos, pobres diablos.

Volveremos reales. No como ahora,
fantasmas en la luz deshabitada.
Volveremos al mundo en que aún no estamos.

Sin conclusión

El transporte del alcohol y de la hierba
nos enseñan que el dios vive en la tierra
y que buscarlo fuera, sería negarnos
a la fascinación de la dicha violenta.

Vamos a la apertura ciega del cero santo
y al éxtasis del tú, ¡oh!, naturaleza.
Lo uno y lo otro son el mismo. Es decir, ninguno existe.
Entonces, ¿de qué hablamos? Las palabras no sirven,

salvo para decir que todo es nada
y que los irreales normalmente existentes
procuran, cuando chocan, el vacío,
y el éxtasis del pleno derramarse y del exceso.

*From *Poemas órficos*.

La Salvaje alegría

Rodeado de dioses y demonios
en esta soledad insoslayable,
sólo Orfeo me asiste y me comparte.

Los que sin maldecir ni rezar, adoramos
los poderes ctonianos, la primavera negra,
el aire libre y el suelto oleaje en las costas,

*From *Poemas órficos*.

We shall return. So distinct
that perhaps we won't recall
the poor devils we were or are.

We shall return as real. Not as we are now,
ghosts in uninhabited light.
We shall return to a world where we don't yet exist.

Without Conclusion

The rapture of alcohol and herbs
shows us the god lives on earth,
and to seek him beyond would deny us
the thrill of violent pleasure.

Let's approach the blind opening of the holy zero,
to the ecstasy of the you, nature.
One and the other are the same: neither exists.
Of what do we speak? Words don't work

except to say that all is nothing
and that the normally unreal existents,
colliding, attain the void
and the ecstasy of excess and overflow.

Savage Joy

Surrounded by gods and demons
in this inescapable solitude,
I have only Orpheus here with me.

We who without curse or prayer
adore chthonic powers, the black spring,
the waves pounding the beach, the open air,

su perfume marino, su podre estimulante,
estamos siempre solos frente a los hombres tristes,
violentos, vacíos, rebeldes para nada.

El poeta está solo. Salvaje es su alegría,
increíble su dicha si no es para los dioses,
y si algo le acompaña sólo es lo femenino

robado a las Bacantes, furiosas, adorables.
Aún en el mismo infierno, dilo tú, mi Euridice,
que olvidando a tu Orfeo te ausentas dulcemente.

Pánica

Sin conciencia colectiva, sin pánica conciencia,
presos en su sagrada personalidad,
sin ver nada más allá,
los enanos mentales rabian, lloran:
"¿Quién como yo? Los robots
pretenden robarme mi individualidad."

¡Pobre Unamuno,
pobres encarcelados en su yo,
ciegos, sordos, mudos, mecos, sin conciencia del total
que es la vida y la alegría de la unanimidad,
el crecimiento glorioso—hombres, nubes, aire, mar—
que ignoran los encogidos en su personalidad!

*From *Poemas órficos*.

El Hombre está solo

Punto en alto:
El instante fulminante,
el momento irrepetible,
el acto

*From *Poemas órficos*.

the exciting smell of the briny rot,
are always alone facing sad men
who are violent, empty, rebels without cause.

The poet is alone. Savage is his joy,
incredible his happiness if not for the gods;
and if something accompanies him it's only the feminine

stolen from the Bacchae, adorable, mad.
Still in the same hell, say it yourself, my Eurydice,
that forgetting your Orpheus you sweetly disappear.

Panicky

Without a collective consciousness, without a panicky
        consciousness,
prisoners in their sacred personality,
not seeing anything beyond,
the mental dwarfs rage and cry:
"Who is like me? The robots
try to rob me of my individuality."

Poor Unamuno,
poor beings incarcerated in their own egos,
blind, deaf, mute, dark, without consciousness of the all
that is the life and joy of unanimity,
the glorious growth—men, clouds, air, sea—
that those shrunk in their personalities ignore.

Man Is Alone

This above all:
The explosive instant,
the unrepeatable moment,
the act

en el que coincide lo increíble con lo exacto.

Y, extendida, abajo,
la primavera negra,
la muerte que da vida,
el coito
de los dioses-animales con las sagradas tinieblas.

Sólo el hombre,
cierta sonrisa inerme,
la frágil desnudez de su belleza
y el miedo
muestran en dónde está realmente el secreto.

Lenguaje cósmico

Todos hablamos con todos: Los pinares con el mar,
los grillos con las galaxias, las yeguas con el Sudeste,
la brisa con lo que calla, las nubes con lo que vuela.
Pero el hombre, distraído, sólo habla consigo mismo.
¿Qué le dice el oro al yodo? ¿Qué, la libélula al toro?
¿Qué los números, al cielo? ¿Qué, la música a la noche?
Porque todos somos partes de un secreto colectivo
pero el hombre, distraído, sólo habla consigo mismo.

*From *Penúltimos poemas*.

La Estirpe común

Y si nos asesinamos, ¡qué significa, hermano,
la sangre derramada en nuestra casa?
Que la vida y la muerte son comunes, hermano,
y que sólo un aliento nos une en los indistinto.
Y nadie podrá nunca distinguir quiénes fuimos,
ni decir quién fue santo sacrificado
o quién ejecutor de un divino mandato.

*From *Penúltimos poemas*.

wherein the incredible coincides with the exact.

And, spread out below,
the black spring,
the death that gives life,
the coitus
of the animal-gods with the holy dark.

Man alone,
the certain defenseless smile,
the naked fragile beauty
and the fear
reveal where the secret really is.

Cosmic Speech

We all speak with each other: the pine groves with the sea,
the crickets with the galaxies, the mares with the Southeast,
the breeze with what is quiet, the clouds with what flies.
But distracted man speaks with himself alone.
What does gold say to iodine? The dragonfly to the bull?
The numbers to the sky? The music to the night?
For we all take part in a collective secret,
but distracted man speaks with himself alone.

Our Common Roots

And if we kill each other, brother,
what is the meaning of the blood spilt in our home?
That life and death belong to all,
and with a final single breath we merge into one.
And never will anyone distinguish who we were,
nor tell which was the holy sacrifice
and which the executor of the divine decree.

Porque no somos tú, ni yo quienes actuamos
sino sólo un nosotros ferozmente sagrado.

¿Humanismo?

El trueno subterráneo, la luz escondida
y en medio nosotros, simplemente humanos.
Primavera negra, cielo sin medida,
y en medio, nosotros, niños, recitando
las tablas que enseñan a multiplicar,
las tablas que enseñan a moralizar
y otras muchas tablas de nunca acabar.
Porque somos niños buenos, humanistas,
salvo a la hora sana y loca de jugar,
y vivir naturalmente, y burlar al mandamás.

*From *Penúltimos poemas.*

Los Dioses terrenos

Eso es la Poesía: Vivir despierto en lo alto
y ver en lo sencillo lo que es extraordinario,
y en lo extraordinario, la evidencia misma,
y en lo cotidiano, la verdadera magia,
y en los oficios, no técnica, milagros.

Eso es la Poesía. No buscar siempre lejos
lo que está en nuestro mundo, lo que está a nuestro lado,
pues los dioses, si existen, tan sólo son terrenos,
y esas luces que a veces parecen detectables
muy lejos, siempre lejos, tan sólo son fantasmas
con los que no es posible charlar de nuestras cosas.

*From *Penúltimos poemas.*

For it is neither you nor I who act
but rather a fiercely sacred we.

Humanism?

The subterranean thunder, the hidden light,
and in the middle ourselves, simply human.
Black spring, measureless sky,
and in the middle ourselves, children,
reciting the tables that teach us to multiply,
reciting the tables that teach us to moralize,
reciting other tables again and again.
For we are good children—humanists—
except at the sane-crazy hour of play,
when we live naturally,
and laugh at the big boss.

The Earthly Gods

That is Poetry: living at the peak of alertness
to see the extraordinary in the simple,
the obvious in the extraordinary,
the magical in the daily,
and miracles—not technology—in work.

That is Poetry: not seeking afar
what is in our world, here at hand,
for the gods, if they exist, are but earthly gods,
and those lights we sometimes discern far away
—always far away—are only ghosts
with whom we cannot discuss our affairs.

Title Index

152

Title Index